*Critical Guides to French Texts*

129  Malraux: La Condition humaine

*Critical Guides to French Texts*

EDITED BY ROGER LITTLE, WOLFGANG VAN EMDEN, DAVID WILLIAMS

# MALRAUX

# La Condition humaine

**Christopher Shorley**

Senior Lecturer in French
Queen's University Belfast

Grant & Cutler Ltd
2003

© Grant & Cutler Ltd 2003

ISBN 0 7293 0438 8

DEPÓSITO LEGAL: V. 272 - 2003

Printed in Spain by
Artes Gráficas Soler, S.L., Valencia
for
GRANT & CUTLER LTD
55-57 GREAT MARLBOROUGH STREET, LONDON W1F 7AY

# *Contents*

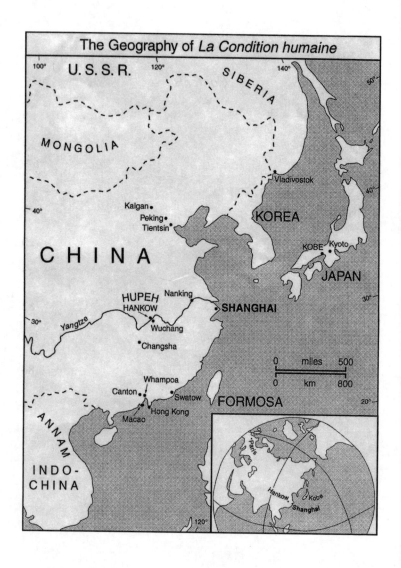

The Geography of *La Condition humaine*

## *Prefatory Note*

All references to *La Condition humaine* are to the Gallimard 'Folio' edition, first published in 1971. Italicized numbers in parentheses, followed by page references, refer to items in the select bibliography at the end of this volume.

The novel's contents are presented in tabular form at the end of my text, before the select bibliography.

I should like to place on record my thanks to Roger Little, the editor, for his constant support and encouragement. I am also very grateful to the following for their help: Gill Alexander, Florence Gray, Marion Khorshidian, Evelyn Mullally, Maura Pringle, Deborah Shorley, Tony Feenan.

I wish to thank The Queen's University of Belfast for funding the preparation of the map.

# 1. CONTEXTS

'L'œuvre d'art survivante nous atteint dans un double temps qui n'appartient qu'à elle: celui de son auteur et le nôtre' (5, p.16). Malraux's claim is vividly illustrated through his own best-known work. Ever since its first publication in 1933 *La Condition humaine* has continued to involve, inspire, challenge and disturb the millions who have read it. If it speaks compellingly of the interwar years in which he wrote, the novel equally attracts audiences in later decades, living in increasingly remote worlds and responding in ever more diverse ways. But from the outset *La Condition humaine* provoked radically divergent reactions. While some early reviewers readily understood its appeal, even a reader as sympathetic as André Gide — like countless others since — was initially put off by its extreme density: the text, he noted in his *Journal* on 10 April 1933, was 'touffu à l'excès, rebutant à force de richesse et presque incompréhensible à force de complexité'. And there have always been objections on aesthetic or ideological grounds. In any case Malraux would argue that categorical judgments are beside the point: that, in the last analysis, 'il ne s'agit pas de rendre une œuvre intelligible, mais de rendre sensible à ce qui fait sa valeur' (6, p.312).

*

Malraux was uniquely caught up in the dramatic history and volatile culture of his own time, and shows an exceptional awareness of them in his writing. 'Une vie dans le siècle', the subtitle of Jean Lacouture's standard biography, neatly captures the coexistence of one individual's evolution and the events of the public, temporal sphere. Gide was dubbed 'le contemporain capital', but the epithet suits Malraux even better. The apparently stable and dominant Europe into which he was born at the beginning of the twentieth century soon gave way to a new world order. A Great War, generated by friction between European states, gradually spread its disastrous effects around the globe; and in its aftermath authority and influence drifted away: to the United States, now militarily and industrially a world power, and to Russia, where the Communist revolution of 1917 had enshrined the rising political creed of Marx and Engels to create a new, theoretically egalitarian, worker-led model of the state. China was emerging from centuries of isolation, the dynamism of Japan was beginning to make itself felt, and soon the peoples of colonized territories would seek to assert their identities and claim independence. Technology was everywhere, constantly increasing the rate of change and altering the quality of experience. The already vulnerable West experienced a further massive trauma following the New York stock market crash of 1929. If the United States was the first to suffer, within a year or two the repercussions — declining trade and growing unemployment — were felt through the interconnected capitalist economies of an emerging global system. In Europe the mood turned to one of crisis and panic, giving rise to political extremism. Italy had had an all-fascist parliament by 1926; Stalin controlled a totalitarian Soviet Union by the early Thirties; and 1933 saw Hitler installed as National Socialist Chancellor of Germany. Politics was unavoidable in a world seemingly poised between Fascism, nationalism and colonialism on the Right, and Socialist, pacifist and liberationist movements on the Left. Spain was torn apart along these lines between 1936 and 1939, and the pattern of conflicts — military and ideological — would continue during World War II and beyond.

For Malraux and his contemporaries, coming to adulthood at the end of the First World War, old dogmas and comfortable certainties were rapidly being discredited — and not only by wartime horrors. Christianity — faced with mounting opposition ever since the Enlightenment — had latterly suffered the critique of Nietzsche, who in the 1870s and 1880s denounced its servility and celebrated the potential of a humanity without God. Equally, the late-nineteenth-century principles of logic and scientific enquiry were questioned by Bergson, while Freud presented human nature as dominated by elements beyond rational control — fantasies, neuroses, sexuality. A new sort of creature was emerging in a changed environment of brutal mechanization and anonymous masses, and traditional explanations could not cope. The Western world as a whole, declared Paul Valéry in 1919, was as 'mortal' as every preceding civilization; the German historian Spengler in *Decline of the West* (1918–22) detected irreversible decay. Increasingly Europeans looked outside their own continent for reference-points, some — such as Romain Rolland — seeing Asian culture as preserving transcendental values lost to materialism and individualism at home. The emerging interwar world is an ever more complex and cosmopolitan place, in which disparate cultures and ideas meet and interact as never before.

By the early 1930s there was clearly, in France anyway, a wide gap between those whose outlook had already been fixed prior to 1914 and those reaching intellectual maturity thereafter. On the one side stood, for instance, Gide, still, in a diary entry for 29 December 1932, reluctant to take a stand on contemporary issues:

> Que l'art et la littérature n'aient que faire des questions
> sociales, et ne puissent, s'ils s'y aventurent, que se
> fourvoyer, j'en demeure à peu près convaincu. Et c'est
> bien aussi pourquoi je me tais depuis que ces questions
> ont pris le pas dans mon esprit.

On the other, the protagonist of a 1934 Drieu la Rochelle story announced impatiently: 'Je suis contre les vieux.'[1] A further split, reflecting developments in the world at large, was gradually assuming greater importance. The younger generation, who sought radical remedies for the ills of the age, themselves divided between those like Aragon or Nizan, who saw salvation in collectivist socialism or communist revolution, and others such as Drieu or Brasillach, who identified with the authoritarian and nationalist positions of the extreme Right. The pressure to confront contemporary events grew ever stronger. In Malraux's words, 'ce qui nous

---

[1] Pierre Drieu la Rochelle, *La Comédie de Charleroi* (1934) (Paris, Gallimard, Folio, 1982), p.104.

distinguait de nos maîtres [...] c'était la présence de l'histoire' (*28*, p.9).

History in one form or another was rarely absent from the life of Georges André Malraux, who was born in Paris in 1901, and died at Verrières-le-Buisson in 1976. The nature of his activities is proof enough: anticolonial journalism in French Indo-China in 1925–26; tireless campaigning against Nazism in the early Thirties; service in a Republican air squadron in the Spanish Civil War; combat in the French Resistance; politics, in General de Gaulle's postwar cabinet and as a Gaullist propagandist; eleven years as Minister for Cultural Affairs at the beginning of the Fifth Republic. Malraux's persona, however, is as much a gallery of images — authentic and fictitious — as of historical roles. He can be viewed as an intrepid explorer during his archeological expedition to the Cambodian jungle in 1923, as an international statesman conferring with Nehru and Chairman Mao, or as the quintessential media intellectual. And behind the outward appearances is an outstandingly original and eclectic mind, formed outside established academic institutions, nourished by voracious reading and a passion for all forms of artistic creation, and open to esoteric influences — the German Romantics, say, or Japanese painting — as much as Cubism, American fiction or Expressionist cinema. Over his career Malraux drew on all kinds of means of expression: film to portray the Spanish Civil War in *Sierra de Teruel*, platform speeches for political causes, ceremonial orations to honour the great. But at the centre of his achievement is a formidable body of prose writings — novels, stories, studies of the visual arts, criticism, essays in autobiography — spanning six decades. When, shortly before his death, he was asked in what guise he would appear to a future generation — writer? revolutionary? politician? art-critic? — he replied without hesitation, 'as a writer, inevitably'[2]

Most of Malraux's writings, like most episodes in his life, offer some reflection of their time. After *Lunes en papier* (1921) and *Royaume-Farfelu* (started in 1920, published in 1928), in which the

---

[2] Olivier Todd, 'Malraux par Malraux', *Le Nouvel Observateur* (3–9 novembre 1975)

eternal themes of destiny and death are treated in a fantastical manner reminiscent of Surrealist texts of the Twenties, *La Tentation de l'Occident* (1926) considers a post-war Europe shattered by war and undermined by the failure of conventional values. *La Tentation* is framed simply as an exchange of philosophical letters between a young European traveller and his Chinese correspondent, but the books which follow — *Les Conquérants* (1928) and *La Voie royale* (1930) — are full-scale works of fiction, addressing Malraux's concerns in unequivocally novelistic form. *Les Conquérants*, set during the 1925 uprising in Canton in southern China, presents the positions of representative figures — a hard-line terrorist, a Gandhi-like spiritual leader, a disciplined Bolshevik cadre — but centres on Garine, the head of propaganda for the Chinese nationalists. Garine, who works for the revolution without ultimately believing in it, is a 'conqueror' — an individual capable of subjecting the world to his will; but sickness and death deny him any eventual sense of triumph or meaning. The impact and immediacy of the text owe much to the unobtrusive first-person narrator, the use of the present tense, cinematic devices and an edgy, telegrammatic prose style. *La Voie royale*, with its Cambodian location, is the second in Malraux's 'Asian cycle'. Its young French adventurer, Claude, whose quest for Khmer statues resembles Malraux's own in 1923, is a companion to the central character, Perken, another embodiment of the will, who in a revealing phrase states his desire to 'laisser une cicatrice sur la carte'. This is a third-person narrative, flexible enough to move between different points of view. Again the style is strikingly innovative: visual effects, such as the view through binoculars, allow dramatic shifts of perception; and elaborate networks of imagery — jungle, insects, blindness, slavery — lend force and substance to a terrifyingly alien setting. Once more the project ends in failure and death, when Perken, having confronted the wilderness, defied hostile tribesmen and rescued a former comrade, succumbs to a poisoned wound, and loses his unequal struggle against fate.

*La Condition humaine*, conceived and written between September 1931 and May 1933, and covering a further stage in the Chinese national revolution, is the last of the Asian series, but its very title announces its wider scope. This novel, technically far more complex than its predecessors, stands as a profound and inclusive statement, extending Malraux's existing themes and pointing forward to all his subsequent work. Like *Le Temps du mépris* (1935) — an affirmation of Communist fraternity — and *L'Espoir* (1937) — Malraux's panorama of the early stages of the Spanish Civil War — it tests out ideologies and actions at times of personal and historical crisis. And like his final novel, *Les Noyers de l'Altenburg* (1941), it serves as an arena for ethical and philosophical debate. Albeit in a less developed form, its notion of art as a means of transcendance anticipates the aesthetic meditations of *Les Voix du silence* (1951); and its essential concern with the identity of the self prepares the way for *Le Miroir des limbes* (1967–75), the reminiscences based on Malraux's own life. More importantly still, *La Condition humaine* continues to reach out from the immediate confines of Malraux's creative work to communicate with new readers, wherever they might be.

## 2. HISTORY

Where Malraux claims that his generation was marked out by the 'presence of history', Jean-Paul Sartre specifies key incidents impinging on their experience: 'A partir de 1930, la crise mondiale, l'avènement du nazisme, les événements de Chine, la guerre d'Espagne, nous ouvrirent les yeux.'[3] The post-Wall Street depression, the rise of Hitler, and civil war in Spain are obvious enough subjects, repeatedly reflected in writing about the period — including Sartre's own. It was, however, Malraux more than anyone else who drew attention to China, which gave him the images of violence and heroism he needed: 'Je les ai trouvées dans les rangs des communistes chinois, écrasés, assassinés, jetés vivants dans des chaudières.'[4] Malraux is no slavish chronicler of Chinese history, nor even an eyewitness. He had only limited first-hand knowledge of the country when he wrote the novel, and did not visit Shanghai until September 1931, well after the events it covers. Moreover his method is usually to insinuate information through terse and elliptical allusions, rather than hold up the narrative to convey it comprehensively. At the same time, the historical situation as he describes it is largely accurate, and provides a frame of reference to underpin the text as a whole.

By the 1920s China is no longer the 'sleeping' nation of which Napoleon supposedly talked. In the words of Gisors, the Chinese 'se sont éveillés en sursaut d'un sommeil de trente siècles dont ils ne se rendormiront pas' (p.332). It has been suggested that they underwent the equivalents of the Reformation, the French Revolution and the Russian Revolution all at once. The major foreign trading nations exercised increasing political influence from the 1840s onwards.

---

[3] Sartre, *Qu'est-ce que la littérature?* (Paris, Gallimard, Idées, 1964), p.257.
[4] Marius Richard in *Toute l'édition* (9 décembre 1933), 1.

During this period they acquired territorial concessions, where they could conduct their own affairs, in Hong Kong, Canton and elsewhere. This explains the early mention of concessions in Shanghai (p.28; the 'huit nations' are Britain, the United States, France, Japan, Italy, Belgium, the Netherlands and Spain; for more details of international trade in the 1920s, including the Stevenson Restriction Scheme to control the price of rubber, see pp.212–13). The Manchu or Qing dynasty, which had ruled its empire from Peking, the northern capital, since 1644, was too enfeebled to resist the foreign powers, despite the resentment of the Chinese people, demonstrated in the Boxer Rebellion of 1900. Equally Peking could not control feudal rivalries or check the revolts regularly taking place in remote provinces of a vast territory. China's ancient society, ill-equipped to handle change, appears in the text in the shape of the 'très vieux Chinois', 'cramponné à son passé', dressed in his embroidered robe, and demanding respect for ancestral attitudes, including the subjugation of women (pp.58–59; see also May's comments on 'l'état des femmes ici', p.48).

When the dynasty finally collapsed, in 1912, a republic was declared and a government formally put in place. However, the real authority now lay with regional military factions headed by so-called warlords such as Tchang Tso-Lin (p.44), who often collaborated with Western powers, and committed numerous atrocities, such as the destruction of Kalgan, in the north (p.65). At the same time a coherent, reforming nationalist movement was gaining ground. A nationalist party, eventually known as the Kuomintang, founded in 1911 by the progressive intellectual Sun Yat-Sen (pp.86, 197), established itself sufficiently to form a rival government in the south, based in Canton, in 1921. On Sun's death, in 1925, the leadership of the party passed to General Chiang Kai-Shek (first reference p.29), who swiftly moved to extend the power of the Kuomintang, launching a military Northern Expedition against the warlords in the summer of 1926. But parallel with the rise of Kuomintang, another force was coming into play, first outside China, then within. Following Marx's *Communist Manifesto* of 1848, proclaiming the historic mission of a revolutionary proletariat to sweep away capitalism, left-wing ideas gradually gained currency. From modest beginnings at the First Workers' International in London in 1864, Communism was coming to prominence by the turn of the century. It had its failures, as in the Crimea in 1905 with 'l'attaque — puérile — de la prison d'Odessa', for which Katow was imprisoned (pp.19, 40). But Lenin's Bolsh-eviks took power in Russia after the October Revolution of 1917 (pp.138, 145–46), overcoming the 'Whites' loyal to the Tsar (pp.73, 266), resisting foreign intervention as at Leningrad (p.142), and controlling internal opponents through a secret police force, the Cheka (p.127). For a time in the 1920s the new Soviet state set about developing its international influence — a policy promoted by Trotsky, but eventually abandoned by Stalin. With the active encouragement of the Third Communist International, or Comintern (pp.124–47 *passim*) started by Lenin in 1919, the Chinese Communist Party came into being in 1921. By 1923 there was a working partnership between the Communists and the Kuomintang. It was based on their joint aim of ridding China of the warlords, but could not eliminate the fundamental differences between, on the one hand, an organization representing a deprived industrial working class and a debt-ridden peasantry (p.68), and on the other, a party of the property-owning bourgeoisie out to reclaim economic privilege. A group of Comintern advisers, led by the Russians Borodin (pp.135, 141) and Gallen (p.143) worked with the Nationalists, first in Canton, scene of the 1925 strike (p.198). By late 1926 Borodin was in Hankow (p.135), where in January 1927 the British were forced to abandon their concession (pp.82, 114, 135).

In 1927 Shanghai is the sixth largest city in the world and China's greatest port, carrying half the country's trade. It has an immense textile industry and numerous Western banks and businesses, and has become a major centre for opium, gambling, prostitution and crime. It is also here that the Chinese Communist Party was founded. 'Cœur vivant de la Chine', this 'ville capitale où se jouait le destin chinois' (pp.116–17) brings together all the major forces bearing on the country's future. Shanghai has, among its cosmopolitan population of over three million, more than forty nationalities, as well as refugees from other parts of China; and it confronts, in a volatile combination, the extremes of luxury and poverty, power and wretchedness: 'chefs de ghildes', 'banquiers', 'directeurs de compagnies', 'importateurs', 'chefs de filatures' (p.116) against 'ceux des filatures, ceux qui travaillent seize heures par jour depuis l'enfance, le peuple de l'ulcère, de la scoliose, de la famine' (pp.23–24). At the beginning of the novel, on 21 March 1927, the city is still officially in the hands of 'Northern' troops. It remains, to a revolutionary such as Tchen, 'possédée comme un champ par son dictateur militaire, louée à mort, comme un troupeau, aux chefs de guerre et aux commerces d'Occident' (p.14). The workers' uprising in February had failed (p.24), but its brutal suppression (pp.39, 40, 82, 104) merely ensured stronger support for another insurrection. Back in February Chiang Kai-Shek and his expeditionary army had not reached Shanghai. Now they are prepared to intervene on their own account, and so destroy the fragile alliance with the Communists. This eventuality is foreseen early on, by Kyo: 'Victoire ou défaite, le destin du monde, cette nuit, hésitait près d'ici. A moins que le Kuomintang, Shanghaï prise, n'essayât d'écraser ses alliés communistes...' (p.48; see also Ferral's projection, p.82, and that of Katow, p.126). Initially the well-organized Communists succeed in taking over the workers' districts (while not attacking the concessions), and the 'Northern' army withdraws on 22 March. However, after Chiang's arrival in Shanghai, the business community strikes a deal with him (p.211). This accords with Ferral's strategy (pp.107–116; historically, the initiative came from the French Consul) — and the fears of Kyo (p.129). The Kuomintang 'bleus' start to pull away from the Communist 'rouges' (p.113; as late as the start of the insurrection, with the alliance still intact, Tchen brandishes the blue Kuomintang flag, p.96). The Comintern denies the Communists the authority to resist Chiang: Kyo's visit to Hankow, where the International is based, confirms Moscow's policy of continued collaboration with the Kuomintang pending an eventual break (p.139). And Kyo is in no doubt of the far-reaching implications for those 'dans toute la Chine, et à travers l'Ouest jusqu'à la moitié de l'Europe' (p.159). From here on the Shanghai Communists are ever more vulnerable. They are already in a minority on the city's newly formed executive committee, dominated by the Right wing of the Kuomintang (p.124); and eventually, on 31 March, Hankow formally orders them to give up their arms (this comes slightly later in the chronology of the novel, p.198). The repression is rapid: Chiang's soldiers take over the Communist strongholds, such as Chapei (p.252) and mop up resistance in a brief spell of street fighting (pp.257, 269–77). Many of the Communist leaders — those who cannot escape — are arrested and executed. For years to come Shanghai will be controlled by a Kuomintang which has broken definitively with its former allies.

If this is the end of the 1927 insurrection, however, the text points forward to events and situations extending far beyond it. 'La vieille Chine', as May sees, is 'jetée sans retour aux ténèbres avec un grondement d'avalanche' (p.337). The historic, world-wide cataclysm, of which the uprising formed part, will go on. Borodin may leave Hankow for Moscow, apparently defeated, in July 1927 (p.320); but soon will come reports of the first Five-Year Plan (p.330–31); meanwhile Parisian investors will make up lost ground in China through enterprises such as railway construction (p.328). As Kyo had anticipated in Hankow, with everything hanging in the balance: 'Moscou et les capitales d'Occident ennemies pouvaient organiser là-bas [...] leurs passions opposées et tenter d'en faire un monde' (p.148).

Tellingly, Malraux's manuscript shows that he removed a number of historical details from his original version. It is as vital for him to keep history within strict limits as to lend historical substance to his narrative. In this way a judicious compromise is achieved in a text with other underlying principles (*64*, p.109). 'La réalité des événements [...] est soumise au contrôle, sélectif, d'un style et d'une vision' (*1*, p.1279). Or, to invert the order of priorities, Malraux must necessarily embrace 'la dimension mystérieuse qu'apporte l'irréalité de l'art' (*34*, p.41).

## 3. TEXT

Artists of Malraux's generation enjoyed an unprecedented relationship with the art and culture of the past. In the early twentieth century many Europeans had a previously unknown access to other civilizations, recent or remote. More paintings and sculptures were displayed in more galleries; growing audiences attended performances of music and drama, or heard them on the radio or gramophone; literatures and philosophies reached larger numbers of readers through libraries, bookshops, magazines and newspapers. Malraux would talk of 'une internationalisation sans précédent de la culture', and tell an audience 'vous qui êtes ici, vous êtes la première génération d'héritiers de la terre entière' (*1*, pp.272, 273). As never before, the cultural heritage stood as a shared resource, preserved in what Malraux would later call a 'musée imaginaire' of reproductions. But equally, given the horror and destruction of the Great War, the rising generation felt a new urge to reject the traditions of its predecessors. A representative — albeit extreme — case was the wilfully outrageous Dada movement, leading in the 1920s to Surrealism, which took as its inspiration the subconscious, non-rational mind.

The post-war world saw innovation and radical change throughout the established arts — in, say, the music of *les six*, the painting of Picasso and Braque, or the poetry of Cocteau or Jacob. But perhaps the most striking developments appeared in forms just coming into their own, such as jazz, reaching Europe towards the end of the war, and — above all — cinema. Moving pictures had begun only in the 1890s, but within two decades were crossing all national and linguistic boundaries and attracting audiences of millions, to become the first new mass medium since print. Soon, with directors such as Griffith, Murnau and Eisenstein, film was claiming its place as an original means of expression capable of the most powerful effects. In this environment categorical distinctions between art and entertainment, 'high' and 'low' culture, tended to blur, and the role and status of the novel now seemed ill-defined. Pseudo-historical and pseudo-scientific narrative *à la* Balzac or Zola appeared out of phase with modern experience, and their successors — Proust or Kafka — accordingly adopted radically new methods to embrace a rapidly changing world. Breton, in his *Manifeste du surréalisme* (1924) famously quoted Valéry's remark that he could not tolerate an idiom with openings as banal as 'La marquise sortit à cinq heures'. Gide, having ridiculed the Naturalist novel in *Les Caves du Vatican* (1913), created in *Les Faux-Monnayeurs* (1925) a novelist endlessly reflecting on the problems of authenticity and technique — from characterization to plot to realism. The following years brought the influential French translations of Joyce's *Ulysses* (1929) and Faulkner's *Sanctuary* (1933). The series of challenges laid down over this period would be taken up by Gide's successors, including Bernanos, Céline and Sartre — and, in his own unique way, by André Malraux.

*************

From his earliest writings Malraux was alive to contemporary artistic issues. Alongside his fiction, evolving as it does from the whimsical 'farfelu' stories to the letters of *La Tentation de l'Occident* to the novels, is an extensive body of reviews, prefaces and interviews in which he refines his thinking. *La Condition humaine* can legitimately be read as the mature product of this on-going process: the expression of a radical response at a crucial point in the novel's development. Various allusions — to *Alice in Wonderland* (p.120), *The Thousand and One Nights* (p.244) and the stories of E.T.A. Hoffmann (p.257) among others — signal Malraux's sense of a literary inheritance. But increasingly sceptical of what traditionalist critics called 'l'art du roman' — the conventional reworking of an established view of things — Malraux valued instead 'la sensation que notre monde pourrait être différent, que les modes de notre pensée pourraient n'être pas ceux que nous connaissons' (*56*, p.114). More specifically he envisaged a decisive break with the nineteenth-century practice of recounting and explaining from a stable position of knowing superiority ('omniscience'), in favour of 'une métaphysique d'où tout point de vue fixe soit exclu' (*4*, p.152).

The strategic decision to write about events too recent for historical perspective is itself revealing (*Les Conquérants*, published in 1928, covers events from three years earlier; in 1931 Malraux begins a novel set in 1927–28). In textual terms the point is perfectly made by the *in medias res* opening of *La Condition humaine*, where the reader witnesses a murder without receiving any preliminary explanation. Initially the narrative shuttles between the mental processes and physical sensations of the killer, not allowing the reader to stand back and understand but rather offering the chance to live through the event in all its bewildering immediacy. Even when the accompanying facts emerge — the killing has taken place in Shanghai (p.13), and its purpose is to secure a shipment of arms for use in an imminent insurrection (p.14) — they count for far less than the churning of Tchen's stomach and his nervous, fragmented thoughts (p.9), or the blood trickling down his arm, and his agonizing over how to deliver the fatal blow (pp.10–11). Tchen himself does not reflect on the wider concerns for ten full minutes (p.14) — and the reader is denied the possibility. The bland novelistic beginning so despised by Valéry and Breton has been left far behind.

*Prose style and literary manner*

What may at first sight seem to be frustrating disorder in fact follows a coherent creative principle, and on closer acquaintance the uncompromisingly terse opening reads as typical of Malraux's prose. It is not for nothing that Tchen's style of speech will later be singled out, since it has resonances for the whole text: 'Son ton, la structure de ses phrases, avaient [...] quelque chose de bref: il exprimait directement sa pensée, sans employer les tournures d'usage' (p.171). Descriptions are repeatedly streamlined by ellipsis: 'la salle de bar du petit hôtel Grosvenor — noyer poli, bouteilles, nickel, drapeau' (p.161); 'manteau de laine, feutre noir, cheveux blancs: Gisors' (p.259). Similarly a straightforward staccato rhythm effectively conveys speed of thought and action: 'Ces boîtes [...] gênaient [Ferral]. Il chercha en quoi, ne devina pas. Sortit. Rentra, comprit aussitôt' (p.222). The compression is also apparent in Malraux's imagery. Similes are frequent: heavy clouds gather 'comme si d'immenses ombres fussent venues parfois approfondir la nuit' (p.23); or, in a dark Chinese shop, a candle is reflected 'dans les jarres phosphorescentes alignées comme celles d'Ali-Baba' (p.41). But the prevailing drive for concentration is more typically served by metaphor, when comparison gives way to identification: the same night sky thus *becomes* something else as 'une invisible foule animait cette nuit de jugement dernier' (p.25); Clappique, whose voice has been likened to that of the *commedia dell'arte* figure Pulcinello, or Polichinelle (p.29), is *turned into* Polichinelle (pp.29, 35, 36). The underlying importance of metaphor is confirmed by the fact that many instances in the published text are reworkings of similes in earlier versions: 'la nuit bouillonnait' (p.13), for instance, was originally the more tentative 'la nuit semblait bouillonner' (*64*, p.100).

The impulse to compress can also bring together elements which are not merely distinct but actually contrast — or even conflict — with each other in oxymoron, another rhetorical figure characteristic of Malraux. Gisors, alone at night smoking opium, combines negative and positive in 'une désolation qui rejoignait le divin', and visualizes on the lake waters 'ce sillage de sérénité qui recouvrait doucement les profondeurs de la mort' (p.72). Such passages reflect a basic division between the physically perceptible and the purely abstract, and in many cases the contrary elements cannot hold together in one formula, instead pull apart to stand separately. At one extreme the emphasis rests exclusively on the tangible, the data of the senses — explosions, the fires' red glow, the stench of corpses. Experience of this order is strikingly rendered through synecdoche, the trope whereby the whole is identified with just one of its aspects. In the hotel room Tchen is less aware of the arms dealer than of 'ce pied à demi incliné par le sommeil [...] — de la chair d'homme' (p.9); likewise the government troops surrounded by the insurgents — 'les assiégés cachés derrière leurs guichets fermés à bloc' — are reduced to the 'train blindé' with its gun turret, apparently the sole source of counter-attack (pp.122–23); and when, awaiting death in the darkened *préau*, Katow tries to give away his cyanide, 'impossible de voir quoi que ce fût; ce don de plus que sa vie, Katow le faisait à cette main chaude qui reposait sur lui, pas même à des corps, pas même à des voix' (p.307). At the other end of the scale from sensual apprehension and physical phenomena lie abstract concepts. Gisors, incapable of touching the body of his dead son, distances himself by expressing his grief in such an abstraction: ''Toute douleur qui n'aide personne est absurde', pensait Gisors […]. Mais il n'osait pas avancer la main' (p.311). This tendency towards categorical statements and aphorisms is widespread. Much earlier, discussing Clappique's need to find a refuge in alcohol, Kyo shifts into generality, asserting: 'Aucun homme ne vit de nier la vie'; then, speculating on whatever torment it might be that drives Clappique, he continues: 'Tout homme ressemble à sa douleur' (pp.45–46).

Taken to the limit, abstract formulations in the manner of, say, La Rochefoucauld's *Maximes*, run counter to the nature of the novel, which has inevitably been to capture the specific and the contingent. In *La Condition humaine*, however, a balance is maintained by the sharp focus on anecdotal, material detail. The generalizing tendency will find fuller expression elsewhere — most of all, perhaps, in *Les Noyers de l'Altenburg*, whose main protagonist, Walter Berger 'retrouvait d'instinct le tour aphoristique de sa conversation et de ses cours: la discussion crystallisait toujours sa pensée' (*2*, p.680). Along with Tchen's language, whose extreme terseness is so deliberately emphasized, Walter's style shows strong affinities with its creator's. In both cases the effect is to enrich the text rather than denature it, for both belong to a wider pattern of eclecticism. In Malraux's hands the novel is an inclusive, heterogeneous form, bringing together the most diverse material. When, for instance, the insurgents check the discs containing secret messages, not only are their actions described, but the abrupt sequence of words and sounds they hear is reproduced (pp.20–21). Modern technology insinuates itself again when the rhythm of a face-to-face conversation is disrupted by the telephone. Ferral, in the midst of questioning the Shanghai police chief, takes a call, and his side of the exchange alternates with suspension points representing the words of the caller (p.84). Later Ferral's negotiations with a Kuomintang envoy and Liou-Ti-Yu, the banker, are repeatedly interrupted by telephone reports on the progress of the uprising (''*La gare du Sud est tombée.*' [...] *Les ponts sont pris.* [...] *Le train blindé est isolé*' (pp.107–15). And König, Chiang Kai-Shek's security chief, systematically exploits incoming calls to intimidate Kyo during his interrogation (pp.287–88). Letters — of course, a major feature in narrative fiction for centuries — had formed the substance of *La Tentation de l'Occident*. Malraux particularly admired Laclos's epistolary novel *Les Liaisons dangereuses* (1782) (7, pp.334–42), and there may well be an echo of Laclos's Madame de Merteuil in the scornful, witty letter in which Valérie mocks Ferral, her erstwhile lover (pp.217–18). The impact is the greater because, by its very nature, the letter denies Ferral an immediate response, while continuing to resound as a devastating insult. But there are other such insertions, less dramatic than Valérie's, but always varying the texture and the dimensions of the narrative: the note which a drunken Clappique writes to himself in a state of near-schizophrenia (p.259), Chpilewski's message about Clappique's statues (pp.263–64), or Peï's account of his life — and Hemmelrich's — since the uprising (pp.329–30). Still smaller textual fragments are used in the same way: the document specifying — devastatingly — that the *Shan-Tung* arms are '*payables à livraison*' (p.18), the banners stating the claims of the striking factory workers (p.79), or Kyo's annotation of a text by Gisors (p.313).

Ferral also reads through a recent speech by Chiang Kai-Shek setting out his attitude to the Communists in the Kuomintang (pp.85–86), and here the novel goes beyond textual collage towards the border with another category of writing, drawing on the methods of newspaper journalism, with its necessary anchorage in historical figures and contemporary events. Soon after publishing *La Condition humaine* Malraux speculated about 'une nouvelle forme de roman' on this model, arguing that 'la force virtuelle du reportage tient à ce

qu'il refuse nécessairement l'évasion, à ce qu'il trouverait sa forme
la plus élevée […] dans la possession du réel par l'intelligence et la
sensibilité' (*56*, p.117). The use of datelines at the beginning of
sections of narrative — an explicit rejection of traditional chapter-
headings — is a further mark of what Malraux would later call the
'nouvel imaginaire: celui de l'événement, chaque jour renouvelé par
la presse' (*5*, p.189). Malraux's radical thinking about the novel
draws on other emerging influences, too. He was among the first in
France to recognize the importance of contemporary American
fiction in the early 1930s. His preface to the French edition of
*Sanctuary* famously described Faulkner's novel, with its
confrontation of helpless character and arbitrary destiny, as
'l'intrusion de la tragédie grecque dans le roman policier' (*36*, p.97).
Even earlier the blurb for *Les Conquérants* had talked of an
'atmosphère de roman policier' (*64*, p.92), and Malraux took a
particular interest in Dashiell Hammett, whose 'hard-boiled' thrillers
such as *Red Harvest* appeared around 1930 and were rapidly
translated into French. In *La Condition humaine* the assassination of
the arms dealer (pp.9–15), the hijacking of the arms shipment
(pp.72–77) and Hemmelrich's killing of the Kuomintang soldier
(pp.273–77) could all be scenes from this topical, popular form, just
as the abruptness of the narrative and the modern urban setting — 'la
rue, la vitesse et la violence' (*5*, p.190) — are all entirely in keeping
with it.

## Other artistic effects

'Pauvre romancier pour qui le roman serait *seulement* un récit' (*8*,
p.333). For Malraux, certainly, the novel is not merely a narrative in
words, but an interface with other forms of expression, other areas of
artistic endeavour, traditional and contemporary. There are perhaps
symbolic reasons for gathering the Communist insurgents together in
a Western-style record shop (p.17), and it is particularly fitting that
when Kyo seeks out Clappique at the *Black Cat*, the prevailing mood
is set by a jazz band: 'une ivresse sauvage à quoi chaque couple
s'accrochait anxieusement' (p.28). Clappique's story-telling is set
against all-enveloping bursts of sound and intervals of pervasive

silence: 'd'un coup [le jazz] s'arrêta' (p.28); 'un coup de cymbales furieux [...] et la danse recommença' (p.30); 'le chahut du jazz cessa' (p.33). Malraux's own rhythm thus takes on the sharp alternations and jarring contrasts of an aggressively modern form of music and dance.

But if jazz makes one significant intervention in the text, the visual arts are a frequent presence. On the white walls of Gisors's house hang 'des peintures Song, des phénix bleu Chardin', and at the end of the hall stands 'un bouddha de la dynastie Weï, d'un style presque roman' (p.43); Ferral's apartment has 'des Picasso de la période rose, et une esquisse érotique de Fragonard' and a Buddhist statue of 'une très grande Kwannyn en pierre noire, de la dynastie Tang' (pp.108–09): two miniature 'musées imaginaires' within Malraux's creation. Kama, Gisors's brother-in-law, is a painter, one of whose 'lavis' or wash drawings adorns Ferral's *fumerie* (p.231); and Clappique deals in paintings (pp.109, 119, 188–89). Further, the visual arts repeatedly offer a field of comparison. Ferral's graceful Chinese courtesan is likened to a Tang statuette (p.231); and when a solidly built Flemish prostitute approaches Clappique, he thinks of seventeenth-century portraiture: "Un Rubens [...] mais pas parfait: elle doit être de Jordaens" (p.245).

But it is assimilation — rather than mere reference — which has the greater impact. As in Cubist painting there is strong emphasis on stark geometrical shapes, such as the blocks of light made by windows and doors (pp.9, 255, 311), and powerful linear effects: black horizontals of barbed wire (p.273) or the vertical bars in the cells when Kyo is first imprisoned (pp.279–84). Elsewhere clean lines and sharp demarcations can be effaced in the manner of Chinese landscape painters, when the streets of Shanghai reduce to a blur as Tchen prepares to explode his bomb: 'La brume, nourrie par la fumée des navires, détruisait peu à peu [...] les trottoirs pas encore vides [...]. Enfoncés en perspectives troubles, les énormes caractères se perdaient' (p.234). Similarly the casino is dissolved into splashes of light and colour reminiscent of an Impressionist interior 'dans une brume de tabac où brillaient confusément les rocailles du mur, des taches alternées — noir des smokings, blanc des épaules — se penchaient sur la table verte' (p.239).

The object of attention is sometimes isolated by being explicitly framed, as if it were a portrait or landscape in its own right. Kyo dwells on May's face in the mirror as she plays with her Pekinese (p.49), then stares bitterly at his own, half-caste features (p.52); likewise a troubled Tchen interrogates his reflection in the lift after the murder (p.15), and Clappique talks to himself, 'le nez touchant presque la glace' (p.258). Ferral can look out from a 'vaste fenêtre' over a whole city in ferment: 'Le soir de guerre se perdait dans la nuit. Au ras du sol s'allumaient des lumières' (pp.115–16). At Comintern headquarters in Hankow there is a reverse effect when another large window, with the starry night sky behind it, forms a vivid backdrop to the confrontation — visual and ideological — of Vologuine the Party ideologue and Tchen the assassin: the one standing with arms folded, the other holding his head in his hands, and both reluctant to speak (pp.142–43). Perhaps the most memorable framing device is that which captures the final image of the one central character to be seen in death: 'Dehors, la nuit; dans la pièce, la lumière de la petite lampe et un grand rectangle clair, la porte ouverte de la chambre voisine où on avait apporté le corps de Kyo' (p.311). Here, as in much Western painting, Malraux combines framing with the technique of lighting, which is also exploited in the description of a shop interior: 'Dans cette brume sale brillaient sur les panses des lampes-tempête des effets de lumière, points d'interrogation renversés et parallèles' (p.184). Lighting gives a range of sculptural, even tactile possibilities, capable as it is of lending its subjects both substance and texture. In the opening scene the only illumination — the harsh electric light from a neighbouring block — falls on the sleeping man's bed, and the shadow of a window-bar is cast just above his exposed foot 'comme pour en accentuer le volume et la vie' (p.9). There is another chiaroscuro when Hemmelrich, at the beleaguered Communist Party offices, sees his comrades scrabbling for hand grenades 'dans la pleine lumière des lampes', and is struck, above all, by 'le volume de ces corps épais' (p.256). The impression has particular force when a human face — Ferral's — is haloed against the surrounding darkness, as if in a de La Tour painting: 'Gisors regarda ce visage aigu aux yeux fermés, éclairé du dessous par la petite lampe, un effet de lumière accroché aux moustaches' (p.227) — a vision of human striving which will persist in Gisors's memory until the end of the text (p.335). Light seems not so much to transform the world as to abolish it when Clappique walks away from the casino and the moon appears through the clouds: 'Sa lumière de plus en plus intense donnait à toutes ces maisons fermées, à l'abandon total de la ville, une vie extra-terrestre' (p.244). But it is the climactic scene of the *préau* which gives the motif of light its richest set of associations. The 'atmosphère nocturne' (p.296) completely obscures the detail of the setting, as in Goya's *The Madhouse*, one of the pictures most precious to Malraux; and as night draws on, the only light comes from a lantern on the floor, itself reminiscent of another work by Goya, *The Execution of the Third of May*. Finally, after the death of his comrade Kyo, and the gift of his cyanide to his comrades, Katow is led off to be executed, and his dark shape assumes the greatest intensity at the very moment when he disappears for ever:

> Comme naguère sur le mur blanc, le fanal projeta l'ombre maintenant très noire de Katow sur les grandes fenêtres nocturnes; […] lorsque son balancement se rapprochait du fanal, la silhouette de sa tête se perdait au plafond. Toute l'obscurité de la salle […] le suivait du regard pas à pas. (p.310)

## Cinematic effects

The sight of faces appearing and disappearing as a lamp sways overhead (p.17) may pass for just one more instance of painterly 'effets de lumière', but in its reorganisation of space it equally suggests more modern, technological models. Katow before the attack on the *Shan-Tung*, and Kyo travelling upriver both suppress distance using binoculars (pp.75, 133–34), and Chiang Kai-Shek, otherwise remote and invisible, enters the narrative in the form of a photograph (p.211). But along with the traditional plastic arts the dominant visual influence on Malraux is cinema. He was fascinated by a medium which had grown up exactly when he did, and which, in the early Twenties, he had hoped to promote (*15*, p.43). Later he would discuss its aesthetic and cultural significance in 'Esquisse d'une psychologie du cinéma' (1939), written at much the same time as he made the film version of *L'Espoir*. For Malraux cinema became an art in its own right when, by the editing of individual shots, it could transform space and time: 'Le moyen de reproduction du cinéma était la photo qui bougeait, mais son moyen d'expression, c'est la succession des plans' (*7*, p.327). It is commonplace to seek parallels with cinematic technique in earlier writers up to and including Zola, but in *La Condition humaine* the link is put beyond doubt when, in a fast-moving sequence, Kyo and Katow make their tour of revolutionary *permanences*:

> Ils sortirent, reprirent leur marche. Encore l'avenue des Deux-Républiques.
> Taxi. La voiture démarra à une allure de film. (p.42)

For narrator and reader alike the ambiance of the early gangster movie suggests itself irresistibly. In an early version of Hemmelrich's confrontation with the Kuomintang soldier (pp.273–76) he sees the sinister figure swelling 'comme au cinéma' (*64*, p.99); and the last view of Katow, with his huge shadow spreading out over the ceiling, recalls not just Goya but the dark and monstrous images of German expressionism, as in Wiene's *The Cabinet of Dr Caligari* (1919), to which Malraux specifically refers in the 'Esquisse'. The play of black and white, light and shadow — constant reminders of monochrome early cinema — pervades the text from the darkened hotel room of the opening to the Comintern's brilliantly lit villa to the gloom of the *préau*; and with them go carefully orchestrated alternations of background and foreground, as with Clappique's face, surrounded by the illuminated sign of the *Black Cat* (p.35), or Kyo's first view of Hankow: 'La ville apparut enfin [...] dans les trous d'un premier plan net et noir' (p.133).

Malraux's close-ups are as arresting as those of, say, Eisenstein's *Battleship Potemkin* (1925), also mentioned in the 'Esquisse'. The 'frame', in the cinematic sense, can be completely filled by an obsessive, larger-than-life image, such as a hand reaching out to grip a strand of barbed wire ('la main se dressa nette et noire, ouverte, les doigts écartés', p.274; the echo of the Hankow 'premier plan' is itself noteworthy); and this is followed by a strikingly similar 'shot' when Kyo arrives in the dark prison cell: 'Il ne voyait que des doigts énormes crispés autour des barreaux' (p.280). Valérie first appears, anticipating sexual pleasure, in an extended smiling close-up — eyes, mouth, and short, wavy hair — (p.118), and May's face, as she imagines being separated from Kyo, is likewise captured in lingering intimacy: 'Sans qu'un seul de ses muscles bougeât, une larme coula le long de son nez, resta suspendue au coin de sa bouche, trahissant [...] ce masque aussi inhumain, aussi mort que tout à l'heure' (p.202). This eminently filmic device is given due emphasis in the 'Esquisse': 'Un acteur de théâtre, c'est une petite tête dans une grande salle; un acteur de cinéma, une grande tête dans une petite salle' (7, p.330). A slightly longer shot simulates a stock comic effect, when Katow, on his rounds, sees 'sous le bras du Chinois qui lui ouvrit la porte, cinq têtes penchées sur la table mais le regard sur lui' (p.37). Sometimes it is camera movement which creates the effect, as in the pan which follows May's pointing finger to sweep across the hills surrounding Kobe (p.333), or the tracking shots as Ferral's car passes through the crowd (pp.79, 87), and the chimneys of Hankow come into view (pp.133, 135).

The increasing versatility of the cine-camera is one important change occurring between Malraux's early experiences of cinema and the writing of *La Condition humaine* in the early 1930s. The most far-reaching development, however, was the transition from silent film to sound, 'talkies' being widespread by 1929 and firmly established within three or four years. Ever alive to technical innovation, Malraux was to comment: 'La puissance d'expression des sons enregistrés, assez faible tant que seuls la transmettaient le disque et la radio, devint très grande quand elle trouva dans l'image son contrepoint. [...] Le cinéma sonore est au cinéma muet ce que la peinture est au dessin' (7, p.329). The novel's noisy 'soundtrack' frequently assimilates effects typical of the early 1930s: strident car horns (pp.9, 86) or the clatter of trucks bouncing over uneven road (pp.78, 106). But if sound often serves to support the images on the screen, it can also draw in events set at a distance from the immediate action. As they mobilize their comrades in the Chinese city, Kyo and Katow can hear the whistles from the launches on the river (p.23); Ferral's negotiations with a Chinese banker are interspersed by the distant gunfire from the armoured train (p.114); and the conversation of a poverty-stricken European couple overheard by Clappique puts his own situation into perspective (pp.291–92).

Simultaneous events are elsewhere covered in successive sequences: Clappique, for instance, stays at the casino from 11.15 until one o'clock in the morning (pp.237–43), after which there is movement back in time, with Kyo and May waiting for him at the *Black Cat*, as arranged, at 11.30 (p.248). Here, though, Malraux is drawing not on the practices within 'plans' or shots, but on editing or montage, whereby the component shots are organized according to a narrative structure. Soon after completing *La Condition humaine* he would write of contemporary literature specifically in terms of the arrangement of visual events: 'En termes de cinéma, je dirais qu'à côté d'une littérature de photographies commence à se constituer une littérature de montage' (63, p.86). The ellipsis or montage cut, particularly emphatic in early cinema where the screen turns briefly dark between shots, lends itself particularly well to a text so marked by discontinuities of all kinds. This most obviously promotes the contrast between episodes of intense physical action and those of meditation and intellectual debate. A more sustained example is the shift from Clappique in a bar-room conversation with the police officer Chpilewski ("Il faut que je prévienne le jeune Gisors', pensa-t-il') to Tchen by the river preparing his assassi-nation attempt (p.165) then back to its previous subject ('Clappique avait pensé trouver Kyo chez lui', p.187). But elsewhere montage can make for continuity — most obviously in the device of *fondu enchaîné*, whereby an image or motif fades at the end of one shot only to reappear at the beginning of the next, as when the small boat on a tranquil lake in Gisors's reverie turns into the revolutionaries' launch on the choppy waters of the river (p.72).

*Scenes*

Whatever the nature of the novel, Malraux argues in the 'Esquisse', the novelist

> est amené à raconter — c'est-à-dire à résumer, *et* à mettre en scène — c'est-à-dire rendre présent. J'appelle mise en scène d'un romancier le choix instinctif ou prémédité des instants auxquels il s'attache et des moyens qu'il emploie pour leur donner une importance particulière. (*7*, p.331)

For all Malraux's affinities with cinema, 'mise en scène' has wider implications. It was understood from classical times that the narrative text included a strand of dramatic representation, and the French novel, from, say, Madame de la Fayette to Proust gives increasing prominence to sequences which can readily be assimilated to theatre. In Malraux's crisp distinction 'la narration exprime un passé dont la mise en scène — en scènes — fait un présent' (*14*, p.96). For an anthology of extracts from his novels, he chose the title *Scènes* (rather than the more usual *Pages*) *choisies*. Just as symptomatically, in his preface to *Sanctuary* he suggested that Faulkner's starting-point may well have been scenes rather than characters: 'Je ne serais nullement surpris [...] que l'œuvre fût pour lui non une histoire [...] mais bien, à l'opposé, qu'elle naquît du drame' (*36*, p.96). It is no surprise, then, if Malraux worked in a similar way, building up his narrative from a series of blocks which can appropriately be called 'scenes' in the theatrical sense (*56*, pp.121–22). Even typographically, in a text not conventionally divided into chapters, the vast majority of sections are clearly demarcated in time, through headings which serve as 'stage directions'. The unity of the scene is further confirmed through the strong sense of place. Just as arresting images can be 'framed', so crucial sequences are meticulously 'staged'. While linking passages regularly allow movement through the open expanses of streets, alleyways or the river, delimited spaces are consistently used to concentrate atmosphere and heighten tension. The arms dealer's dark hotel room, the shadowy little shops, Ferral's modern apartment and Gisors's Chinese bungalow are all integral to the events which occur in them. The importance of physical enclosure is particularly marked in the final fraught scene between Kyo and May. As they argue in the bedroom May deliberately blocks the doorway to prevent Kyo from walking out (p.200), standing aside only when the argument has run its course (p.203). When Kyo initially goes without her, the shutting of the inner and outer doors seems to symbolize a definitive separation (May even listens for an imaginary third door to close), but the intensity of the moment in the room proves too strong: Kyo is compelled to return to find May as he had last seen her, and the couple leave together (p.205). The larger-scale drama of the *préau* scene, too, is worked out precisely in terms of entrances and exits, from the soldiers bringing in the lanterns ('La porte s'ouvrit', p.298) to the last sight of Katow ('la porte se refermait', p.310).

Malraux's use of space and movement goes further, detailing individuals' actions and gestures, and 'stage business' in general. Clappique's first appearance, in the *Black Cat*, is not merely histrionic in a general sense, but unfolds as a performance — a 'spectacle' (p.44) — through his clown's voice 'inspirée de Polichinelle' (p.29), his well-rehearsed body-language ('les coudes au corps, gesticulant des mains, il parlait avec tous les muscles de son visage en coupe-vent', ibid.) and a stand-up routine running the gamut of styles from 'confidentiel' to 'plaintif, sanglotant' to 'scientifique' to 'éploré' to 'doctoral' (pp.29–32). There is a chilling counterpart to this display when a drunken Clappique, teetering on the brink of madness, will literally pull faces in the mirror 'se transformant en singe, en idiot, en épouvanté [...] en tous les grotesques que peut exprimer un visage humain' (p.258). The most highly charged scenes are all given substance by theatrical means. The sequence of May's confession to Kyo insists on faces, eyes opening and closing, and contrasting postures: Kyo hunched miserably on the bed, May staring out of the window (pp.50–52). The chance encounter between Tchen and the missionary, Smithson, has them walking arm in arm and looking into each other's faces — until they are separated by what amounts to a piece of street theatre (pp.165–69). And the whole scene in the *préau* is played out via the attitudes and moves of the guards and the wounded prisoners, the tantalizing fumbled exchange of the cyanide, and Katow's majestic exit. Before his arrest, Katow visits the wretched Hemmelrich, and the sympathy he cannot put into words finds another outlet: 'Par des paroles, il ne pouvait presque rien; mais au-delà des paroles, il y avait ce qu'expriment des gestes, des regards, la seule présence' (p.210). Even when speech is possible, the unspoken can still undercut it. At the end of his final conversation with his son Gisors 'essaya de sourire; Kyo aussi, et leurs regards ne se séparèrent pas: tous deux savaient qu'ils mentaient, et que ce mensonge était peut-être leur plus affectueuse communion' (p.199).

## Dialogue

In any and all of the languages to be heard in *La Condition humaine* words prove cruelly inadequate and frustratingly elusive. Tchen cannot verbalize his ideals — even in Chinese (pp.150, 185); and Katow, seeing his condemned comrades weeping, bitterly reflects: 'Y a pas grand-chose à faire avec la parole' (p.306). But in a text drawing so extensively on cinematic and theatrical presentation, dialogue inevitably has immense significance. Noting that, after all, 'une pièce, ce sont des gens qui parlent' (*7*, p.329), and that film directors had eventually succeeded in integrating dialogue, Malraux insists that 'le dialogue essentiel: celui de la scène' marks out every major novelist. It is, he argues, 'le grand moyen d'action sur le lecteur, la possibilité de rendre une scène *présente*' (*7*, pp.331). Like the aphorism or the letter, dialogue has long been a form of literary expression in its own right, for example in the Socratic tradition or Diderot; and it was to be central to *Les Noyers de l'Altenburg* — and to Malraux's autobiographical writings. In *La Condition humaine* the speaking voice is systematically juxtaposed with silence, as in the

Paris sequence or the *préau* scene, at the end of which 'le silence
retomba, comme une trappe' (p.310). The voice itself is a minimum
guarantee of human presence: Kyo hears Clappique as a 'voix
singulière dans l'obscurité, quand ne la soutenait plus aucune
expression du visage' (p.36), and Clappique perceives the
insubstantial, mist-shrouded beings outside the casino as 'pas même
des ombres: des voix dans la nuit' (p.241). But it serves also to
individualize: Hemmelrich's voice sounds 'presque haineuse' (p.22),
and Ferral's is clipped and mechanical (p.83), while Kyo clings
desperately to May's essential characteristic: 'la douceur de sa voix,
encore dans l'air' (p.54). Beyond which the frequent references to
accent and pronunciation (particularly for Tchen and Katow) and tics
and mannerisms (notably those of Katow, Ferral and Clappique) all
confirm the importance of direct speech (*66*, pp.48–53). Often this
means nothing more than the most laconic of utterances — terse
questions and answers, orders, threats. Sometimes a speaker prefers
the sound of his own voice to exchanges with others: Clappique's
comic patter, or König's obsessive monologue about his torture in
Siberia, which reduces Clappique himself to silence (pp.266–67).
But the text depends greatly on the detailed conversations which bear
on contingent and immediate events: the council of war before the
uprising (pp.17–23), Ferral's various discussions of the prospects
(pp.81–86, 108–11, 111–15) or König's attempt to recruit Kyo
(pp.286–90). More crucial still is the series of substantial debates,
distanced from the heat of the action, in which different positions are
articulated and confronted, as when Gisors and Tchen discuss the
ethics of killing (pp.59–64), Ferral and Valérie engage in a
sophisticated verbal joust about masculinity and femininity
(pp.119–20), Smithson challenges Tchen's political 'faith'
(pp.166–69), or Clappique interrogates Kama's artistic principles
(pp.189–92). And at the very heart of the novel is the philosophical
dialogue between Ferral and Gisors (pp.225–30). Tellingly, the
narrative ends not with events or actions but with the final
conversation between Gisors and May (pp.331–38). The text is a
thing of diversity, a combination of fragmentary and contrasting
elements rather than the privileging of any single, consistent voice.

## Point of view

'Le roman longe la frontière des formes; on l'admire au nom
d'analogies avec elles (composition, force, ordre, style), mais il leur
échappe, d'abord par sa fluidité' (*5*, p.193). Here Malraux turns
away from the novel's common boundaries with other media and
genres to stress its inherent distinguishing qualities. He argues that
the modern novel came into being precisely when it freed itself from
the requirements of oral narration, as practised in, say, early
medieval romance. Regardless of the crucial role of dialogue,
'comment imaginer un grand roman où le romancier ne pouvait
s'adresser directement au lecteur que par la *voix* de ses
personnages?' (*5*, p.304). Or, to reverse the logic of the declaration
in *Les Voix du silence*, 'pauvre romancier pour qui le roman *ne serait
nullement* un récit'. The novelist — and the novel — are necessarily
defined by the choice of narrative voice. Malraux had before him
two obvious precedents: the self-confident, pseudo-objective third-
person — or heterodiegetic — narrator typical of the mid-nineteenth
century, and the more recent homodiegetic methods of Gide and
Proust, based on a clearly subjective first person: the voice of a
character involved in the narrative. In his first two novels Malraux
had settled on relatively straightforward methods, both avoiding
traditional 'omniscience': the discreet, anonymous 'je' of *Les
Conquérants*, close to but separate from the main protagonist, and
the restricted third person of *La Voie royale*, sharing the narrative
focus between the two central characters. Later the more complex
*L'Espoir* would bring together numerous different viewpoints in
what one critic calls a 'récit hybride'. Technically — as
chronologically — *La Condition humaine* stands between the earlier
works and the later one. While rarely seeking to attract attention as in
Balzac or Stendhal — addressing the reader directly and stating
opinions — a heterodiegetic narrator does appear occasionally. This
can provide background information — in an explanatory footnote
(pp.27, 42, 212, 287) or when, before the uprising, Katow meets a
*tchon*: 'une des organisations de combat communistes que Kyo et lui
avaient créées à Shanghaï' (pp.37–38). It can also add details beyond
the knowledge of the characters themselves, as when Gisors cannot

understand Ferral's state of mind (p.227) or Clappique's agitation (p.260), or is too preoccupied to hear May (p.336); and when Kyo and May are knocked senseless, it is only this independent narrator who can explain that the attack is the work of Chiang Kai-Shek's police (p.251). In composing the novel, however, Malraux systematically shifted information and observation away from the external narrator (*64*, pp.85–86), and the final text is predominantly narrated from the standpoint of the characters themselves. During the Paris meeting the minister announces: 'Je laisse à M. Ferral le soin de [...] présenter son point de vue' (p.316). While he uses the term loosely, simply looking to Ferral to argue his case for the Consortium, the whole sequence is indeed seen through Ferral's eyes, as he notices the expression on the officials' faces (p.315), catches one of them staring at his undecorated lapel (p.319), and studies the minister's profile (p.324). And Ferral not only sees but reflects, so that the sequence also reads as an alternation between his visual perceptions and his thoughts. These are signalled lexically, through the repetition of terms such as 'songer', 'comprendre', 'penser' and 'réfléchir' (pp.316–27), and conveyed in either the present ('N'écoutez, pensait-il, que votre courage', p.320) or *style indirect libre* ('Ils ne paieraient pas [...] parce que Ferral n'était pas des leurs', p.321). This direct access to characters' mental processes also covers memory, as when Ferral recollects an anecdote about the minister (p.316), and in this way the narrative regularly reaches back into the past. Gisors will recall Tchen's childhood in the attempt to understand his current situation, stressing the importance of memories more generally (pp.64–68). And in this he will be echoed by Katow ('Comment veux-tu qu'on comprenne les choses autrement que par les souvenirs...', p.207) — Katow who is haunted by the traumatic memory of facing a firing squad in Lithuania (pp.73–74).

Malraux's narrative draws on various parts of the subjective mind at work, especially those which deviate from neutral, stable consciousness: Tchen's neurotic dread of the dreams which assail him (p.149), or Kyo's utter shock at the brutalizing of the madman in prison: 'une horreur toute-puissante avant même que l'esprit ne l'eût jugée' (p.284). Hemmelrich's discovery that his wife and child have been hideously killed sets off a burst of irrational responses: 'Une exaltation intense bouleversait son esprit, la plus puissante qu'il eût jamais connue; il s'abandonnait à cette effroyable ivresse avec un consentement entier' (p.254). 'Bouleversement' and drunkenness are also central to Clappique's mental processes (pp.243, 257–59). But a still more fundamental reordering occurs in the slow-motion, out-of-focus musings of Gisors, late at night after his fifth pipe of opium: 'Les objets [...] se perdaient: sans changer de forme, ils cessaient d'être distincts de lui, le rejoignaient au fond d'un monde familier où une bienveillante indifférence mêlait toutes choses' (p.71). Despite — or because of — May's infidelity, Kyo's perceptions are momentarily taken over by raw sexual desire (pp.54–55); and Kyo's experience at this point, like Clappique's at the roulette table, is so intense as to blot out all other areas of his consciousness in what seems like the onset of death — 'comme vers une agonie' (p.55) in one case, 'comme s'il eût attendu après avoir avalé un poison' (p.243) in the other. Elsewhere simile gives way to physical experience. Blown apart in his abortive attempt to assassinate Chiang Kai-Shek, Tchen dies in a paroxysm of pain: 'Il prenait conscience de la douleur, qui fut en moins d'une seconde au-delà de la conscience [...]. Rien n'existait que la douleur' (pp.235–36). Having taken his cyanide capsule, the suffocating Kyo 'sentit toutes ses forces le dépasser, écartelées au-delà de lui-même contre une toute-puissante convulsion' (p.305).

The diversity of the narrative owes much to the extremes of consciousness, but even more to the extensive range of points of view. While Ferral is the focalizer in Paris, the opening scene is recounted entirely through Tchen, switching between simple narrative discourse, direct and indirect speech. Tchen will also be used as focalizer on other occasions, as at the start of the uprising, where the precise limits of his field of vision are specifically pointed out: 'La fumée qui sortait lentement par la fenêtre l'empêchait de voir les insurgés de gauche' (p.96). A significant number of characters will play the same role: Gisors, as in the small hours of 21 March (pp.58–72); Kyo, for example during his visit to Hankow

(pp.133–59); or Clappique at the casino (pp.237–45). Some minor
figures — Martial pondering on Ferral (p.83), Hemmelrich at the
moment of the Kuomintang's victory (pp.273–77) — occasionally
operate in the same way, even if others — Vologuine, Kama, König
— never do. Moreover the viewpoint can shift from character to
character not merely between sequences, but within them. Although
his perceptions dominate the 'quatre heures du matin' sequence in
the first part, Gisors is briefly observed from the outside, by Tchen
(pp.59, 61), and while Tchen is still the central consciousness at the
beginning of the second scene (pp.16–20), after his departure his
function passes to Kyo (pp.22ff.) and Katow (pp.37ff.). In the major
dialogues there is a balance not only between the characters' spoken
words, but also their share of the narrative focus. Valérie's viewpoint
is juxtaposed with Ferral's (cf. 'elle crut', 'elle savait', 'elle sentit'
and 'pensa Ferral', 'il s'imagina', pp.121–22), just as May's
perceptions and Gisors's are counterpointed ('May pensait', 'pensa-
t-elle' as against 'Il sembla à Gisors', 'songea-t-il', pp.334–35). The
*préau* scene has perhaps the most elaborate combination of all.
Initially the point of view is that of Katow, in position to observe
('appuyé sur un coude, Katow [...] regardait', p.296), as he gradually
makes out the bodies of the other prisoners in the gloom, hears and
even smells them, coming finally to understand the hideous end
which awaits, and to feel the fearful anticipation (p.299). The focus
then switches to Kyo, and, given his posture ('allongé sur le dos, les
bras ramenés sur la poitrine, Kyo ferma les yeux', p.302, to the
meditation which precedes his suicide, before returning to Katow,
now forced to contemplate his own mortality. The climax brings a
further shift, as Katow limps towards death, now viewed, in his turn,
by the other prisoners: 'toutes les têtes [...] suivaient le rythme de sa
marche. [...]. Tous restèrent la tête levée' (p.310). This sequence
demonstrates perfectly how the narrative is generated not by any
identifiable authorial voice, nor even a discrete set of privileged
viewpoints. There is, on the contrary, no absolute or definitive
perspective, but rather a thoroughgoing relativism: a multiplicity of
coexisting perceptions; and it is the tension between them which
sustains the entire text.

*Characters*

The novelist's defining liberty in the construction of narrative extends still further:

> liberté que ne limitent nul interprète, nulle narration orale, nulle mémoire, mais seulement la navette entre auteur et personnages, la marge où ceux-ci prolifèrent, inséparable de la conscience qu'a le romancier de ne s'adresser ni à un interlocuteur ni à un spectateur, mais à un lecteur. (*5*, pp.180–81)

Just as the reader of *La Condition humaine* is offered no privileged view of events, so there is no one protagonist on whom a simple plot will centre, but rather a sizeable group of interconnected participants in a complex set of circumstances. Further, Malraux keeps his distance from established modes of characterization — the subtle psychological analysis of Proust, say, or the fictional portrayal of living people in the 'roman à clef'. For him, far from existing in their own right, characters are subordinate to a governing vision of the novel as a whole, as in Dostoyevsky (*34*, p.41), or Flaubert who, 'ne croyant plus qu'un grand roman naisse de grands personnages [...] veut que les bons personnages naissent des grands romans' (*5*, p.121). Malraux's order of priorities is clear — and the scope of character in his own texts remains accordingly limited: 'L'autonomie des personnages, le vocabulaire particulier donné à chacun sont de puissants moyens d'action romanesque, non des nécessités' (*34*, p.38). The characters of *La Condition humaine* are individualized enough to be distinctive threads in the narrative texture, not self-contained, fully rounded entities. Significantly perhaps, very few — Tchen, Kyo, May and Valérie — are even given a full name. The limitations are strongly suggested by Malraux's removing a gripping episode featuring Clappique from the final text because it gave disproportionate importance to this one individual (*19*, pp.74–75). When perceived from the outside, characters are schematically portrayed through perfunctory details, often added at a late stage of composition (*64*, pp.44 ff.): Katow's unbuttoned jersey (pp.23, 37), or Hemmelrich's 'tête de boxeur crevé' (p.17). There are also brief circumstantial notations lending an 'effet de réel', such as the play of light on Peï's spectacles (p.172), or the cigarette case Ferral keeps open on his desk to demonstrate his self-control (p.112).

As schematic 'présences' rather than autonomous 'caractères' (*63*, p.141), the major characters are defined more by the roles they perform within the 'action romanesque'. Most obviously there are those who initiate action: Tchen, who assassinates the arms dealer, leads a section of shock troops and finally attempts to kill Chiang Kai-Shek; Kyo and Katow as coordinators of the uprising; and Ferral, working to organize resistance and protect the Consortium. Others are important precisely for their lack of initiative — notably Clappique, through his failure to save Kyo. Clappique is, rather, a go-between for parties remote from or hostile to each other, and thus unlikely to come face to face. As an art dealer he mediates between Ferral and Kama; and it is he who fixes the rendezvous with the captain of the *Shan-Tung* for the Communists, and tips off Kyo about the Kuomintang's decision to arrest him. Gisors is a still more crucial intermediary, connecting with diametrically opposed figures — Tchen and Ferral, May and the misogynist 'très vieux Chinois'. Moreover Gisors acts as a facilitator, a sounding-board for others ('La pente de l'intelligence de Gisors l'inclinait toujours à venir en aide à ses interlocuteurs', p.63), and as a recurrent influence in their own thinking (p.67 for Tchen, p.151 for Kyo, p.225 for Ferral, p.332 for May). Characters in a third category play purely minor, episodic roles. Neither initiators nor intermediaries, they act as satellites, supporting the major actors — Peï and Souen with Tchen, Shia and Hemmelrich with Kyo and Katow, Martial with Ferral.

Within any given environment, Malraux argues, the novelist has the opportunity to set 'un moment décisif de son personnage' (*7*, p.332), and it is perhaps here that the characters play their most vital part in the action. More important than the summary physical traits are the salient facts of their past lives — Katow's struggles in Tsarist Russia (pp.73–74), Ferral's rise to power (p.85), Gisors's spell as a sociology professor in Peking (p.44). For these act as a necessary backdrop to the crises which the major figures experience individually and collectively in the course of the narrative. At the beginning Tchen's act of murder is the decisive moment when he leaves behind his identity as just one more young intellectual revolutionary; at the end Gisors's loss of his son cuts him off irrevocably from the rest of the world. In between, most major figures reach some comparable turning point — Katow in his final sacrifice, Hemmelrich after his wife's death, and Kyo and Ferral doubly so, since the crisis in their public, social lives as leaders of their organisations runs parallel with another in their personal, sexual relationships.

The subordination of individual character to the overall design of the text becomes clearer as Malraux expands on his view of them as 'de puissants moyens d'action romanesque, non des nécessités'. For him, the primary obligation of the novelist is elsewhere: 'Je ne crois pas vrai que le romancier doive créer des *personnages*; il doit créer un monde cohérent et particulier' (*34*, p.38). Beyond the multiplicity of protagonists, the point is reinforced by the distribution of groups and collectivities — revolutionary cells, night-club society, families, couples. And the huge cast of 'extras' — prostitutes, coolies, factory workers, traders, businessmen, prisoners — sustains the sense of a vast milieu in which individuality is of strictly limited importance. But Malraux's argument leads further. In creating his 'monde cohérent et particulier, comme tout autre artiste', the novelist must meet a more specific need: 'Non faire concurrence à l'état-civil, mais faire concurrence à la réalité qui lui est imposée [...] tantôt en semblant s'y soumettre et tantôt en la transformant' (*34*, p.38). Unlike Balzac, claiming to create characters in imitation of those listed in the register office, Malraux's novelist is to fashion them as constituent parts of the constructed 'world' of his own narrative. It follows that the consistency of character is as much a matter of thematic linkages crafted in the text as of physical or biographical information. When Katow walks to his death ('le fanal projeta l'ombre maintenant très noire [...] sur les grandes fenêtres nocturnes', p.310) he completes a pattern embracing his first appearance, in the phonograph shop ('en arrière, dans l'ombre', p.17), the long shadow he casts on the pavement (p.126), and the image earlier in the *préau* sequence: 'son ombre pas encore très noire qui grandissait sur le mur des torturés' (p.299). May's words 'Je ne pleure plus guère', with which the text closes, signal her determination to transcend her grief at the loss of Kyo, but gain in resonance from earlier events. She speaks just after Gisors has taken her head in his hands and embraced her, exactly as Kyo had done before their final separation (p.203), and just after the close-up of a tear of rolling down her face (p.202). Soon afterwards, tending Kyo's body, she is already beyond tears (p.311). There is also another echo, for when König recounts the torture he underwent in Siberia, he explains: 'J'ai pleuré comme une femme' (p.266). König's entire profile, moreover, is a systematic reversal of Katow's: the first an unwilling prisoner, the second volunteering to join his comrades; König held by the Communists, Katow by the Whites; the one afffirming himself by destroying others, the other sacrificing himself to save them. The same linking process is at work throughout, drawing together distant and apparently disparate elements of the text. Ferral's seemingly gratuitous reflection when he meets a handsome woman on the stairs ('Je voudrais bien savoir la tête que tu fais quand tu jouis, toi', p.86) assumes its full significance only when linked with his subsequent behaviour towards Valérie (p.121). Perhaps the most subtle and pervasive pattern begins when the alley cat creeps up behind Tchen just after the murder (p.13), thereafter to haunt his dreams (p.149). The motif will symbolically disappear from the text through Ferral's allusion to the Cheshire Cat, of which nothing remains but its smile (p.120), but not before both Kyo and Valérie have been compared with cats (pp.41, 120), and likewise Clappique's Philippine prostitute (p.34), in a nightclub whose name is no mere accident.

## Time and space

For Malraux, in the fully constituted novel 'récit' becomes by definition a coherent 'world' in its own right, so there is an inevitable stress on its large-scale extensions in time and space. The importance of chronology is already apparent in the notations of dates and times at the beginning of textual divisions, which conveys an initial sense of consistent and rapid forward movement from the starting point of 12.30 a.m. on 21 March. But, as Malraux was to argue, unless the passing of time is governed by some all-embracing principle, the novel might amount to not an overarching 'durée' but merely a succession of 'scènes' (*64*, p.74). *La Condition humaine* imposes its own sort of time, for the multiplicity and distribution of the characters means that events cannot follow any simple linear progression. From an early stage discrete incidents occur more or less simultaneously. The attack on the *Shan-Tung*, beginning at '4 heures et demie du matin' (p.72) overlaps with the long preceding sequence in Gisors's house. This runs from '4 heures du matin' and covers the departure of the 'très vieux Chinois', the sustained conversation with Tchen, and the meditation when Gisors smokes his five pipes of opium (pp.58–72). But the swift succession of events is counterpointed by periods when the pace is explicitly slackened — in Part Three, after Kyo has spent six unaccounted-for days travelling upriver to Hankow (p.133), or in Part Seven, set first in Paris after a gap of three months, then in Kobe a full year after the beginning, and thus completely outside the foregoing time-scale. An incident in a clockmaker's shop neatly captures the relativity of time: 'Tchen regarda l'heure. […] Trente pendules au moins, remontées ou arrêtées, indiquaient des heures différentes. […]. Il ne pouvait détacher ses yeux de cet univers de mouvements d'horlogerie' (p.125). Time cannot be an unproblematic given. On the contrary its rhythm and intensity must vary with the occasion and the individual — as when Clappique misses his 11.30 rendezvous with Kyo. Having entered the casino at 11.15, he checks his watch at 11.25 (pp.239–40). He is then drawn irresistibly to the roulette wheel, and time in effect ceases to exist for him: 'Pourquoi regarder la montre? Il rejetait Kyo dans un monde de songes' (p.241). When he glimpses his watch by accident, he deliberately puts it out of sight (pp.242–43). He finally leaves at one o'clock in the morning (p.243). Meanwhile Kyo and May are counting every passing minute. They appear, in the next sequence, precisely as Clappique is checking the time in the casino; but against his dilatoriness is set their anxiety: 'Les cinq dernières minutes. Déjà ils eussent dû être partis' (p.248).

When they hurry out, Kyo reads the time with the help of his cigarette-lighter, and discovers he is already late (p.251). This is when they are attacked by the Kuomintang police and Kyo is abducted. His arrest — one of the key incidents of the novel — comes about precisely through the disparity between his sense of time and Clappique's. But the narrative as a whole is a composite of fragmented time-scales and uneven rhythms. Once again the governing principle of complexity and diversity is at one with the minutiæ of the text.

Space, too, is mediated through differing subjective perceptions. For an emotional Tchen, looking down on the city from the hotel room, 'les lumières de minuit [...] palpitaient de la vie des hommes qui ne tuent pas. C'étaient là des millions de vies, et toutes maintenant rejetaient la sienne' (p.13); a cool, disdainful Ferral, at his window, sees 'une foule en mouvement [...]; il lui sembla soudain que l'âme de cette foule l'avait abandonnée' (p.118). At a later stage Ferral looks at a military map of Shanghai 'avec de grandes taches rouges qui indiquaient les masses des ouvriers et des misérables' (p.211), which abstracts a strategic meaning from the geography — as Kyo has already done in preparing the uprising: 'Il avait cessé de voir les rues: il ne marchait plus dans la boue, mais sur un plan. Le grattement des millions de petites vies quotidiennes disparaissait' (p.24). In an altogether different register, Clappique inverts the vastness and gloom of the city in the whimsical conceit of 'ce p'petit village ensoleillé' (p.161). Space — specifically urban space — is thus appropriated and stylized throughout. Discussing his choice of settings Malraux noted: 'Je crois qu'il y a dans une époque assez peu de lieux où les conditions d'un héroïsme possible se trouvent réunis' (*34*, p.2). Whereas the text mentions numerous cities from Vladivostok to Buenos Aires, they are not physical realities but merely insubstantial locations in a global network. Strikingly — and quite unlike Malraux's earlier novels — *La Condition humaine* never represents travel as such, but merely suggests it through the start of Clappique's and Ferral's journey (pp.295–96), and the end of Kyo's (p.133) and May's (p.328). By the same token countryside, river and sea feature only insofar as they mark the outer limits of urban territory.

For Malraux, as for contemporaries such as Dos Passos and Döblin, the metropolis is integral to his text. All the action takes place in four cities, each distinguished in its own way. Portrayed only briefly, in the final sequence, Kobe with its coolies, cars and sirens nevertheless sums up many of the urban motifs established earlier in the text. However, it invests in them a new ambiguity: the possibility of some future reconciliation suggested by a homecoming crowd uniting workers and bosses on a 'veille de fête' (p.335) which reverses Clappique's doleful valedictory on Shanghai ('la fête est finie', p.295). Paris, to which Ferral eventually returns (having never stopped thinking of it, p.88), lies at an intermediate point between Shanghai — which it seeks to exploit — and New York, on which, in economic terms anyway, it ultimately depends. But the Paris of July 1927 is reduced to a Finance Ministry void of detail and material substance: a trivial forum offering Ferral nothing more than the exchange of empty platitudes ('une langue conventionnelle et ornée', p.321), ending up in 'un non-sens total' (p.327). Paris is an abstraction in which Ferral's whole project is liquidated. In parallel it is Hankow which undermines Kyo, who seeks the support of the Comintern. Unlike Paris, however, Hankow has a marked physical presence, albeit one of inertia and inactivity: a direct contradiction of Communist propaganda. The dominant and inescapable image of Hankow comes from the very noise and vibration of the Comintern printing-press:

> Transmis par la terre, le frémissement des machines de l'imprimerie [...] les pénétrait des pieds à la tête [...]. Kyo ne pouvait se délivrer de cet ébranlement de machines [...] — comme si ces machines à fabriquer la vérité eussent rejoint en lui les hésitations et les affirmations de Vologuine. (p.147)

Hankow, then, embodies yet more words in the air, another non-sense. But by any reckoning Shanghai is the dominant city. Far more than the others, Shanghai exemplifies in a very literal way Malraux's dictum about the novel's ability to connect crisis with 'l'atmosphère [...] qui l'entoure' (*7*, p.332). Beyond the street names and exotic architectural details it is precisely the atmosphere, with its pervasive damp, its cloud and lingering mists, which encompasses everything. 'Cœur vivant de la Chine, Shanghaï palpitait du passage de tout ce qui la faisait vivre; [...] les vaisseaux sanguins confluaient comme les canaux vers la ville capitale où se jouait le destin chinois' (pp.116–17). Ferral's metaphor enshrines the notion of convergence — both physical, as in the river he overlooks, flowing from Hankow (p.116), and figurative, in Vologuine's admission that information gets lost 'sur le long chemin de Moscou à Shanghaï' (p.138). But above all it installs Shanghai as the centre — of the novel as of the wider world it represents. The countless conflicts and contrasts, the clashes of personality and ideology, the exchanges of cultures and civilizations, make it an ideal microcosm, perfectly embodying the diversity of the text itself.

## Organization

'Le livre est le résultat d'une élaboration, d'une suite de parties, tantôt gouvernées et tantôt instinctives [...] dans lesquelles le grand romancier trouve une coordination qui lui appartient comme le timbre de sa voix' (*5*, p.148). The work of Malraux's novelist identifies itself at the highest plane of textual organization as in the minutest stylistic detail. As he notes in 'Esquisse d'une psychologie du cinéma', even if the demarcated sequences of a film may correspond to chapters, the overarching structure of parts is a resource particular to the novel (*7*, p.330). Parts are the largest unit in all his novels except the small-scale *Le Temps du mépris*. The earliest of them, moreover, share a common trajectory: an initial upward movement leading to short-term achievement followed by the ultimate failure and death of the main protagonist (*12*, p.29). And the structure is clearly based on a formal division into parts — three in *Les Conquérants*, four in *La Voie royale*. If the dynamic of *La Condition humaine* is more complex, the similarities remain. Parts One and Two convey, with great urgency, the rising curve of the insurrection from its preliminaries to its initial success as Communist fighters — a collective protagonist — take over large tracts of Shanghai. Part Three is a levelling-off, and a distanced overview of events past and to come. The pattern thus far is of 'preparation, action, recapitulation' (*41*, p.50). At the centre of the structure, Part Four balances ascending and descending motion: the potential assassination of Chiang Kai-Shek and the actual death of Tchen. Thereafter, sustaining the symmetry, the curve is emphatically downward. In Part Five Clappique, having earlier been of service to Kyo, now fails him; Kyo, having controlled previous events, is now arrested and rendered powerless; the Communists, besiegers at a previous stage, are now themselves besieged. Part Six completes this progression with the deaths of the leading insurgents and the defeat of those who survive. But *La Condition humaine* also accommodates a further trajectory, integrating as it does the rise and fall of another protagonist, in the person of Ferral. The opponent of the insurrection, and an effective force of reaction in the first half of the text, he is himself finally consigned to defeat through the collapse of the Consortium. After Part Six there is a thoroughgoing dispersal to counterbalance the intense concentration of the earlier stages. All the major survivors from conflict have left Shanghai: Clappique and Ferral aboard the same ship to Europe; Gisors joining Kama in Japan; Hemmelrich, Peï and — eventually — May to work in Soviet Russia. Part Seven constitutes an epilogue quite separate from the preceding narrative — even a negation of what has gone before, given Ferral's realisation that 'tous les événements de Shanghaï allaient se dissoudre', reduced to meaninglessness, and Gisors's parallel recognition that 'le sens de la vie de Kyo' — the only thing he holds dear — is gone forever (p.337).

Outside the parabolic trajectories, and unmarked by the previous thrust of events, Part Seven embodies — precisely in its stasis — a different order of patterning, which can be traced back through the rest of the novel. Its first section pits Ferral against the French financial establishment, but its ultimate outcome — the liquidation of the Consortium — will occur beyond the confines of the narrative. What matters for the text is the very fact of the dialectical tension. Likewise, in the Kobe scene Gisors's weary indifference is juxtaposed with May's determination to continue the revolutionary struggle. Subsequent developments are not part of the text in this case, either: the importance of this final encounter lies in the recurrent play of binary opposites it suggests. And the whole text is shot through with similar patterns. At the very outset Tchen, poised to kill his sleeping victim, glimpses 'sous son sacrifice à la révolution [...] un monde de profondeurs auprès de quoi cette nuit écrasée d'angoisse n'était que clarté' (p.10), thus establishing the interplay which will remain a constant throughout: the visible with the unseen, surface and depth. Inversely, for Clappique as he emerges from the casino, 'tout à coup, à travers ce qu'il restait de brume, apparut à la surface des choses la lumière mate de la lune' (p.244). Gisors sees the duality in an image of his own mind. Looking 'au plus profond de lui-même', he comes to realise that his obvious appreciation of Chinese art 'n'était plus qu'une mince couverture sous quoi s'éveillaient [...] l'angoisse et l'obsession de la mort' (p.70). Later, contemplating even the quintessentially superficial Clappique, Gisors decides that 'au-dessous des attitudes de tout homme est un fond qui peut être touché' (p.262). Tchen's early perception is, equally, part of a further, equally far-reaching set of oppositions. The dark of the hotel bedroom contrasts with the harsh electric light outside; the predominantly nocturnal ambiance in which the uprising is prepared ('les verres de centaines de lampes-tempête [...] se perdaient dans l'obscurité, jusqu'au fond invisible du magasin' (p.26) is followed by the 'soleil provisoire' of its beginnings (p.126); and the deepening gloom of Hankow (from 'la lumière trouble', p.134, to 'la nuit maintenant complète', p.142) by the brilliance of Kobe ('la baie magnifique, saturée de soleil', p.337).

**************

'Le monde cohérent et particulier' of the text owes its coherence and specificity to its contrasts and dialectics as much as to anything else. For it is these essential elements which underlie stylistic technique and narrative presentation. Malraux has reinvested his novelistic inheritance to striking effect. As Christiane Moatti observes, 'En les

faisant coïncider, en les combinant, en les dissociant, cet écrivain
[...] qui explore les zones de liberté laissées par le genre avec toutes
les ressources et les tendances nouvelles, forge un alliage esthétique
sans précédent' (56, p.127). At the same time, a purely aesthetic
construct, however consummate, is itself only part of a larger
concern. As Malraux argues in the preface to *Le Temps du mépris*,
'la valeur d'une œuvre d'art [...] est fonction [...] de l'accord entre
ce qu'elle exprime et les moyens qu'elle emploie' (1, p.776). And
what he writes elsewhere concerning detective fiction applies just as
well to his own novel: 'Limitée à elle-même, l'intrigue serait de
l'ordre du jeu d'échecs — artistiquement nulle. Son importance vient
de ce qu'elle est le moyen le plus efficace de traduire un fait éthique
ou poétique dans toute son intensité' (1, p.1273). Perhaps the only
difficulty here is the use of such a traditional term as 'intrigue' to a
text as radically innovative as Malraux's. But, as R.-M. Albérès
argues, if Malraux's novels are 'devoid of plot' in a conventional
sense, it is precisely because the 'plot' is always the same — and
always called 'la condition humaine' (52, pp.51–52). If the text can
be schematized in architectural terms, Malraux's achievement is 'to
manage the whole 'horizontality' of plot and action while yet placing
the emphasis on the 'verticality' of metaphysical awareness' (60,
p.35). Or, as one of Malraux's contemporaries would have it, 'une
technique romanesque renvoie toujours à la métaphysique du
romancier'.[5] Once again — but in an entirely different way —
'pauvre romancier pour qui le roman serait *seulement* un récit'.

---

5 Jean-Paul Sartre, *Situations I* (Paris, Gallimard, 1978), p.66.

# 4. COSMOS

There are important reasons why, at the time Malraux wrote and published *La Condition humaine*, the role of the novelist was radically changing. Balzac had claimed to be the secretary to French society, and Zola had written an authoritative 'natural and social history' of a family during the Second Empire, but in the early twentieth century the novel's social observation was rivalled and surpassed by the rising discipline of sociology as developed by Weber and Durkheim. Moreover as a means of understanding the human mind, fiction in the Twenties and Thirties was challenged by the discoveries of psychology: 'On avait tenu Stendhal pour un plus grand psychologue qu'Auguste Comte, on ne tiendra pas Joyce pour un plus grand psychologue que Freud' (5, p.189). An older generation of novelists was disappearing. Proust died in 1922 (and the last volume of *A la recherche du temps perdu* appeared five years later). *Les Faux-Monnayeurs* (1925) was Gide's last major work of fiction. And while some tried to perpetuate the social panoramas and psychological perspectives — Martin du Gard with his family cycle *Les Thibault* (1922–40), or Romains in *Les Hommes de bonne volonté* (1932–47) — others tackled newer issues without reference to a traditional world-view. A conservative literary 'Maginot Line' was to prove as inadequate as the military one (built at precisely this period) in keeping out harsh realities.[6] In these circumstances the novel could both record modern experience and respond to the volatile, troubling contemporary world. In default of commonly held beliefs, the responses were extraordinarily varied: Giono denouncing mechanized war and promoting a cult of nature in *Le Grand Troupeau* (1931), and Saint-Exupéry pitting the heroism of pioneer

---

[6] Claude-Edmonde Magny, *Histoire du roman français depuis 1918* (Paris, Seuil, 1971), p.25.

airmen against the menace of the elements in *Vol de nuit* (1931); Nizan's Marxist concerns in *Antoine Bloyé* (1933), and Drieu la Rochelle's nascent Fascism in *La Comédie de Charleroi* (1934). The Catholic writer, Georges Bernanos, stands out given Malraux's championing preface to *L'Imposture* (1928), praising Bernanos's unwavering focus: 'Non seulement l'âme est pour lui l'essentiel de l'homme; elle est encore ce qui l'exprime le mieux.' 'Son don essentiel,' Malraux adds, 'celui qui fait la valeur de ses livres, c'est l'intensité' (*63*, pp.217–18). Bernanos's *Journal d'un curé de campagne* (1936) traces the struggle of a naïve young priest stoically confronting the evils of the world, exemplified in the corrosive indifference of his parish. 'On dira peut-être,' he reflects, 'que le monde est depuis longtemps familiarisé avec l'ennui, que l'ennui est la véritable condition de l'homme'.[7] The exact diagnosis matters less than the terminology, which not only reveals Bernanos's personal preoccupations, but relates him to a major contemporary theme, sounded, for instance, by Bardamu, Céline's protagonist in *Voyage au bout de la nuit* (1932), talking ironically of 'ma condition trivialement humaine'.[8]

## 'La condition humaine'

Malraux's own concern with the place of human beings in the order of things — 'condition' here has its early meaning of 'status', 'position in a hierarchy' — was evident by the time of his third novel. In the essay 'D'une jeunesse européenne' (1927) he pointed to the West's growing self-confidence, due especially to technical progress during the nineteenth century: 'un goût extrême, une sorte de passion de l'Homme, qui prend en lui-même la place qu'il donnait à Dieu' (*4*, 138). But the concluding vision of *La Tentation de l'Occident* is of a postwar humanity in the process of losing its grip: 'tous ces hommes appliqués à maintenir l'Homme qui leur permet de surmonter la pensée et de vivre, tandis que le monde sur lequel il

[7] Georges Bernanos, *Journal d'un curé de campagne* (Paris, Livre de Poche, 1977), pp.6–7.
[8] Louis-Ferdinand Céline, *Voyage au bout de la nuit* (Paris, Gallimard, Folio, 1993), p.249.

règne leur devient, de jour en jour, plus étranger' (*1*, p.101). In Malraux's terms the 'death of God', proclaimed by Nietzsche in the 1880s, had been followed by that of mankind as conventionally understood, and a new question arose: 'Quelle notion de l'homme saura tirer de son angoisse la civilisation de la solitude?' (*4*, 134). The problem is never far away in the novels which follow. Of *Les Conquérants* Malraux would claim: 'Ce livre est d'abord une accusation de la condition humaine'.[9] In *La Voie royale* Grabot, reduced in captivity to a bare minimum of existence, wants to know not the names of his rescuers but something much more elemental — 'Qu'est-ce que vous êtes?' — which leaves Claude, for one, overwhelmed by 'le multiple sens de la question' (*1*, p.456). And Perken, contemplating an absurd death in an Asian jungle, realizes that 'ce qui pèse sur moi c'est, — comment dire? — ma condition d'homme' (*1*, p.448).

When, in Shanghai's Cercle Français, Ferral asks Gisors if it is not typically stupid for a man to die for an idea, the reply gives a clear echo — most immediately of Perken, but also of a sequence of earlier voices: 'Il est très rare qu'un homme puisse supporter, comment dirais-je? sa condition d'homme' (p.228). But in this crucial dialogue the whole issue assumes an unprecedented prominence. It not only sustains a theme vital to Malraux and his contemporaries, but carries powerful resonances from the past: from the 'fragilitas conditionis humanæ' of Saint Jerome to Montaigne's 'chaque homme porte la forme entière de l'humaine condition' to Nietzsche's 'unsre menschliche Stellung'. Lamartine's words seem particularly pertinent: 'Nous croyons plus beau et plus viril de regarder en face le malheur sacré de notre condition humaine que de le nier ou d'en assoupir en nous le sentiment avec de l'*opium*' (*56*, p.99). The most important reference of all, however, is to Blaise Pascal (1623–62), the mathematician and polemicist whose best-known work, the *Pensées* (1670), is a collection of fragments written for an unfinished 'apologie' — or reasoned defence — of Christianity. The formal resemblances between the *Pensées* and *La*

---

[9] Malraux, 'Réponse à Trotsky', *Nouvelle Revue Française*, 211 (1931), p.502.

*Condition humaine* are readily apparent in the arresting aphorisms, dramatic juxtapositions and abrupt questions, as well as the strategic use of dialogue. And at a deeper level there is a compelling convergence of intuition and outlook. Malraux's novel can contain no analogue to the 'Félicité de l'homme avec Dieu': a second part of the projected apologia, in which Pascal seemingly planned to convince his reader of the rewards of Christian belief. But there is a vital affinity with the 'Misère de l'homme sans Dieu', a first part intended to press home the full horror of existence in a barren, unredeemed universe. Pascal was well versed in the recent astronomical discoveries of Galileo and his successors, and repeatedly draws on them in the comments of an interlocutor — an unbeliever familiar with seventeenth-century science. And *La Condition humaine* reflects a remarkably similar view of the cosmos. For all the importance of the novel's geographical location, Malraux acknowledged that 'le cadre n'est naturellement pas fondamental. L'essentiel est évidemment [...] l'élément pascalien' (*34*, p.2), just as he told a critic: 'Vous avez raison de partir de Pascal' (*27*, p.27).

There are close correspondences between the *Pensées* and *La Condition humaine* in the images and motifs used to represent the stark terror to which all human life is subject. Pascal's grim picture retains all its capacity to shock:

> Qu'on s'imagine un nombre d'hommes dans les chaînes, et tous condamnés à la mort, dont les uns étant chaque jour égorgés à la vue des autres, ceux qui restent voient leur propre condition dans celle de leurs semblables, et, se regardant les uns les autres avec douleur et sans espérance, attendent à leur tour. C'est l'image de la condition des hommes. (Lafuma 434/ Brunschvicg 199)[10]

---

[10] *Pensées* references are to the edition of Louis Lafuma: Pascal, *Œuvres complètes* (Paris, Seuil, L'Intégrale, 1963), and to that of Léon Brunschvicg: Blaise Pascal, *Pensées et opuscules* (Paris, Hachette, 1897).

It is hard to envisage a more powerful correlative than Malraux's fictional realization of the image, with the arrested Communists in the *préau* agonizingly waiting their turn to die (pp.296–310). Elsewhere Pascal compares the human situation more explicitly with imprisonment in 'ce petit cachot où [l'homme] se trouve logé, j'entends l'univers' (Lafuma 199/Brunschvicg 72) — which translates, in *La Condition humaine*, into a profusion of prison motifs. Kyo and Katow both end their lives in captivity, having already been marked by the experience of imprisonment — Kyo in the common-law jail (pp.279–90), Katow in the lead mines in Russia after the 'affaire d'Odessa' (p.40). The physical environment is often visualized through motifs of bars and walls. In Kyo's eyes the International Concessions reduce to 'des menaces, des barrières, de longs murs de prison sans fenêtres' (p.24), and the caged creatures — the tiny cricket in the gramophone shop (p.18), the blackbirds Valérie leaves for her admirers (pp.211, 215), or the assorted animals Ferral visits on her (pp.220–23) — are so many more reminders. Imagery often sustains the pattern: Tchen enters terrorist life 'comme dans une prison' (p.65); he and Kyo, facing adversity in Hankow, are bound together 'd'une amitié de prisonniers' (p.148); Clappique leaving for Europe hears the ship's bell 'comme celle d'une prison' (p.296). Pascal offers an equally bleak metaphor of the ultimate reality which completes the human spectacle: 'Le dernier acte est sanglant quelque belle que soit la comédie en tout le reste. On jette enfin de la terre sur la tête et en voilà pour jamais' (Lafuma 165/Brunschvicg 210). The climax of Malraux's drama — as well as the bloody events preceding it — has the same violence, and the same deadly finality.

Malraux appropriates not merely Pascal's images and figures of speech but an entire imagined cosmos — a term he himself used for a novel's essential setting (7, p.332). Pascal's interlocutor — the 'homme sans Dieu' to be won over through dialogue with the apologist — sees before him a terrifying prospect characterized by 'le silence éternel de ces espaces infinis' (Lafuma 201/Brunschvicg 206). Likewise, after the murder, Tchen gazes out into the Shanghai night as 'des étoiles s'établirent dans leur mouvement éternel' (p.13);

when the uprising begins, he contemplates 'le calme infini du ciel gris' above (p.95); in Hankow a sombre Kyo finds himself facing 'les grands espaces de la nuit' (p.149). *La Condition humaine* is overtly set in a vast and timeless space whose elemental forms constantly make their presence felt: its skies, landscapes, seas and rivers, its alternations of day and night, its cycle of seasons. And within this vastness mankind is a negligible entity with no necessary place, no recognized home: existence is gratuitous. Such is the terrible realization of the 'homme sans Dieu':

> Quand je considère la petite durée de ma vie absorbée dans l'éternité précédente et suivante […] le petit espace que je remplis et même que je vois abîmé dans l'infinie immensité des espaces que j'ignore et qui m'ignorent, je m'effraye et m'étonne de me voir ici plutôt que là. (Lafuma 68/Brunschvicg 205)

The revelation finds its way into the thoughts of Clappique, alone in an unearthly Shanghai night 'dans cette atmosphère si peu humaine qu'il s'y sentait intrus' (p.244). The sense of cosmic alienation could scarcely be more complete.

The alienation takes other forms. As well as humanity's position — or lack of one — in the cosmos, there is the question of its place in the hierarchy of what Pascal, at least, might call creation. If man is lost in the immeasurable expanse of the universe, he is equally out of touch with the sphere of microscopic organisms on which all life is based, as the seventeenth century already understood: 'Enfin les choses extrêmes sont pour nous comme si elles n'étaient point et nous ne sommes point à leur égard' (Lafuma 199/Brunschvicg 72, entitled 'Disproportion de l'homme'). Pascal's terse questioning emphasizes the predicament: 'Que deviendra donc l'homme? Sera-t-il égal à Dieu ou aux bêtes? Quelle effroyable distance! […]. Qui ne voit […] que l'homme est égaré?' (Lafuma 430/Brunschvicg 431). In Malraux's text the characters are torn between the lofty aspirations and inevitable baseness which define them equally. As Gisors puts it in the dialogue with Ferral:

'L'homme [...] a envie [...] d'être plus qu'homme [...]. Tout homme rêve d'être dieu' (p.229). But it is not difficult to look back to Ferral in his apartment standing insignificantly next to the Buddhist divinity (p.108) as symbolizing an unbridgeable gap. At the other end of the scale the novel's animal population — its countless horses, dogs, cats, fish, birds, insects — is juxtaposed with the human one, just as the street of the animal sellers is situated just beside Shanghai's European concessions (pp.41, 219). Once again, imagery repeatedly reinforces the theme: Tchen is assimilated to a hawk (p.59), or Clappique to 'un singe triste et frileux' (p.191). Ferral surveys 'une foule en mouvement, millions de poissons sous le tremblement d'une eau noire' (p.118), and even for Kyo terrorists can be 'insectes meurtriers [qui] vivaient de leur lien à un étroit guêpier' (p.152). The effect is strongest with the degrading spectacle of the common-law prison. Kyo reflects first on the guard: 'L'abjection du gardien [...] lui semblait une immonde fatalité comme si le pouvoir eût suffi à changer presque tout homme en bête'. But then his thoughts turn to the prisoners, another variation on debasement: 'Ces êtres obscurs qui grouillaient derrière les barreaux, inquiétants comme les crustacés et les insectes colossaux des rêves de son enfance, n'étaient pas davantage des hommes' (p.282).

For Malraux as for Pascal, man is a creature out of place both in the order of natural creatures ('ni ange ni bête': Lafuma 678/Brunschvicg 358) and in the scheme of the universe ('une sphère infinie dont le centre est partout, la circonférence nulle part': Lafuma 199/Brunschvicg 72). The intense awareness of the cosmos gives *La Condition humaine* a scope which, if expected in an undertaking such as Pascal's, is inconceivable in most works of narrative fiction. On the other hand the theological and polemical focus of Pascal's apology leaves him little opportunity to consider the circumstantial details of 'les royaumes, les villes, les maisons' (ibid.) which are the stock-in-trade of the novelist. At best Pascal offers an abstract, generalized analysis of society: its inbuilt conflicts ('tous les hommes se haïssent naturellement l'un l'autre': Lafuma 210/Brunschvicg 451), its inequalities due to the domination of the 'riches' and 'tous ces grands de chair' (Lafuma 308/Brunschvicg 793), its greed and violence ('la concupiscence et la force sont les sources de toutes nos actions': Lafuma 97/Brunschvicg 334). What Malraux adds, through his novel, is a specific field in which these essential lines of force can be traced. His China reflects ancient times (p.227) but centres on the Shanghai of 1927, with its motor traffic, modern architecture and nightclubs. There is a constant stress on the mixture of cultures, nationalities and languages: 'la civilisation rituelle de la Chine' (p.65) and French high fashion, Norwegian sea-captains and Burmese revellers, and 'une rue de petits bars, bordels minuscules aux enseignes rédigées dans les langues de toutes les nations maritimes' (p.245). The *Black Cat* is a microcosm within a microcosm, with its array of ruined businessmen, dancers and prostitutes — 'ceux qui se savaient menacés — presque tous' (p.28) — all speaking with the same voice, 'comme si tous les êtres de ce lieu se fussent retrouvés au fond d'un même désespoir' (p.37). The menace and despair signify that the essence of society is not so much surface difference as underlying dislocation and discord. The historical situation is of course one of conflict — initially between the forces seeking change and the 'Northern' government, then between Communists and Nationalists within their crumbling alliance. But the killings and widespread violence are part of a whole complex of social divisions, setting tradition against modernity, capital against labour, haves against have-nots. The recurrent model for relationships is a transaction which expresses the opposition and tension between the two sides involved. As Kyo is quick to see, Chiang's position in Shanghai will depend entirely on his ability to strike a deal with a middle class not necessarily sympathetic to him: 'La bourgeoisie ne paiera pas pour rien: il faudra qu'il lui rende sa monnaie en communistes zigouillés' (p.129). And when Ferral seeks to enlist the leading Shanghai banker,

> Liou [...] ferma les yeux, les rouvrit, regarda Ferral avec
> l'œil plissé du vieil usurier de n'importe quel lieu sur la
> terre:
>
> — Combien?
>
> Cinquante millions de dollars. (p.114)

In other words the political and military conflict is entirely subject to
the implacable mechanisms of economics and commerce, of which
money is the most obvious outward sign. Shanghai is not only a
meeting point of races and civilisations, but also China's main
banking centre, which attracts all the major financial interests. This
explains the presence of Ferral's Consortium Franco-Asiatique with
its power to transform whole continents, and its concomitant
vulnerability to commodity prices and currency rates — 'ces
poussées de l'économie mondiale' (p.214) — which link Shanghai
with those epicentres of Western capitalism, Paris and New York
(p.213). And the threat of a financial 'krach', apparent to Ferral, the
Parisian bankers and the Finance Minister (pp.212–13, 318, 322), is
perhaps even more obvious to an author writing during the post-Wall
Street crisis. But beyond the large-scale dealings taking place in the
historical context of Shanghai in 1927–28, *La Condition humaine* is
permeated by bargaining and negotiations of all kinds: haggling over
the price of arms (pp.35–36), bribery (pp.93–94, 157, 280), the trade
in works of art (pp.36–37, 119, 188–89). Clappique's career is a
telling paradigm: 'La part de la nécessité est faite par les courtages
d'antiquités, les drogues peut-être, le trafic des armes' (p.46). The
central role of money in even the unlikeliest of situations is vividly
captured in the common-law prison, when Kyo learns that the guard
has spared him in the hope of a reward: ''L'argent me poursuit
jusque dans cette tanière', pensa Kyo' (p.282). Much is made of the
buying and selling of animals — and, equally, of the trade in human
flesh, given the taxi-dancers and prostitutes, and Kyo's ex-mandarin
cell-mate who baldly states: 'Je vends des femmes' (p.280). In the
economy of the text, relationships tend to represent exchange value
rather than intrinsic worth. The inevitable result is another alienation

— in the social sphere — to set alongside that of humankind in the natural universe.

The model of bargaining and negotiation extends still further, as a fundamental process in interpersonal behaviour above and beyond commercial transaction. Thus König explicitly offers Kyo a deal — a 'marché' — to turn informer (p.289). National culture reinforces the pattern, as in the discussions between Possoz and the dissident Hankow dockers: 'Malgré les pistolets, les menottes, Kyo sentait se préparer l'atmosphère de marchandage chinois qu'il avait si souvent rencontrée dans la révolution' (pp.154–55). In the scene between Tchen and the antique dealer, bargaining becomes an activity in its own right, regardless of its material outcome. The dealer, disconcerted by Tchen's preoccupied manner, persists as much for the ritual of social exchange as for financial gain, convinced that 'le marchandage est une collaboration, comme l'amour' (p.173). The financial outcome is subordinate to the interaction between partners, albeit partners with different — even contradictory — motives, and whose pacts are never better than fragile and temporary. Coincidentally or not, the dealer surmises that Tchen wants to buy a present for 'quelque serveuse ou fausse geisha' (ibid.). 'L'amour' in the dealer's scheme of things can certainly take on its widest range of meaning, including relationships of the most loveless kind. Tchen admits that his first sexual experience — with a prostitute, in traditional Chinese fashion — left him with a 'terrible' feeling of separation (p.62), and much the same could be said of Ferral's evening with the courtesan from Nankin Road (p.231–33). Clappique's encounter with a Flemish waitress, despite the genuine sympathy between them, exposes the unbridgeable gap between her humdrum thought-processes and his tall stories (pp.245–48). Kyo acknowledges 'la misogynie fondamentale de presque tous les hommes' (p.54), but May reproaches him with failing to respect a woman's viewpoint (pp.53, 199). More permanent couples, indeed, are subject to the same disaffection: Katow wantonly neglecting a sick wife (pp.208–10), or Hemmelrich trapped in a dispiriting marriage (p.181). In the liaison between Ferral and Valérie — short-lived but precisely detailed — the divisions lead to out-and-out antagonism. Her initial hope of genuine affection ('elle était sa maîtresse pour qu'il finît par l'aimer', p.117) founders on his cruelly reductive psychology ('se donner, pour une femme, posséder, pour un homme, sont les deux seuls moyens que les êtres aient de comprendre quoi que ce soit', p.120). She nevertheless excludes any workable contract between the sexes: 'Ne croyez-vous pas, cher, que les femmes ne se donnent jamais (ou presque) et que les hommes ne possèdent rien?' (ibid.). And it is Valérie who brings the deal to an end: 'Je me refuse autant à être un corps que vous un carnet de chèques. [...] Je suis *aussi* ce corps que vous voulez que je sois *seulement*' (p.218). Little wonder that Ferral dreads the conventions of courtship: 'de l'échange où il payait en importance donnée à une femme ce qu'elle lui donnait en plaisir' (p.224).

Apparently less problematic relationships are prey to the same endemic incompatibility. At the end of a comradely conversation with Hemmelrich, Katow is 'frappé [...] de constater combien sont peu nombreux, et maladroits, les gestes de l'affection virile' (p.210). More starkly, Tchen, forming a human chain with his fellow revolutionaries, feels absolutely separate from those on either side of him, 'malgré l'intimité de la mort, malgré ce poids fraternel qui l'écartelait' (p.105). In these cases what separates individuals is not a difference of aims but the sheer impossibility of mutual understanding. Tchen's late-night visit to Gisors gives rise to a lengthy meditation on the young man whose mentor Gisors has been, and to the question of whether he really knows Tchen at all (pp.59–69). Far more troubling for Gisors is the realization that he has come to know less and less about Kyo: 'Pour la première fois, la phrase qu'il avait si souvent répétée: 'Il n'y a pas de connaissance des êtres', s'accrocha dans son esprit au visage de son fils' (p.65). Given that Gisors is pre-eminently equipped to empathise with others ('son intelligence toujours au service de son interlocuteur', p.225), this is a clear sign of a further level of separation and alienation. Tchen's simple but devastating admission: 'Je suis extraordinairement seul' (p.60) could, at one moment or another, be echoed by any of the other characters, just as all are distanced by the same pervasive vocabulary of 'séparation' and 'éloignement': Kyo from Gisors (p.70), Ferral from Valérie (p.121), and — as late as their final scene together — Kyo from May (pp.200–01). As Gisors puts it, there is a desperate reality in 'l'angoisse d'être toujours étranger à ce qu'on aime' (p.226). In the social universe of Malraux's novel, separation is the norm: by their nature human beings do not belong together.

If the union between individuals is perpetually at risk, the integrity of the self is no more secure. Grabot's unnerving question, 'Qu'est-ce que vous êtes?', is implicit throughout the text. The repeated use of disguises serves to undermine external appearances — Katow and Kyo dressed as government soldiers (p.72), Tchen and his comrades as office-workers (pp.166, 169), or the fugitive Clappique ('Il suffit d'un costume [...] pour trouver une autre vie dans les yeux des autres', p.294). And the vulnerability of the human body itself is regularly emphasized, as in the physical humiliation of König (p.266), or the hideous destruction of Hemmelrich's family (p.253). The body can also be the outward sign of a divided identity: when Kyo first appears 'la lampe marqua fortement les coins tombants de sa bouche d'estampe japonàise; en s'éloignant elle déplaça les ombres et ce visage métis parut presque européen' (p.17). With Kyo, given his Franco-Japanese parentage — 'métis, hors-caste, dédaigné des Blancs et plus encore des Blanches' (p.68) — specifically racial and cultural factors come into play. But by virtue of their upbringing, education and whatever has brought them to Shanghai, all the principal figures are in some sense displaced persons, misfits forever at odds with their environment and themselves.

The tension between outer and inner is regularly demonstrated by characters literally confronting their own image. When Tchen catches sight of his reflection in the lift, 'le meurtre ne laissait aucune trace sur son visage... Ses traits [...] n'avaient pas changé' (p.15): appearance does not necessarily square with experience. A guilt-ridden Clappique, by contrast, conducts a reproachful dialogue with the 'Clappique du miroir' and drunkenly tries to simulate his feelings in dumb-show (pp.258–59). In a disembodied way Clappique also hears his own laugh, thus underlining the disparity between mental and physical experience. But the crucial instance occurs in the gramophone shop when Kyo is convinced, on first hearing, that his sound recording has been altered. As is explained, he like anyone else fails to recognize his voice because he is used to perceiving it only from the inside, through his own body, instead of with his ears (p.21). This startling notion of a complete and irreparable split between subjective and objective perception reverberates throughout. It comes back to Kyo in the *Black Cat* (p.31), is picked up by Gisors (p.47), and is again recalled by an increasingly troubled Kyo: ''On entend la voix des autres avec ses oreilles, la sienne avec la gorge.' [...]. 'Mais moi, pour moi, pour la gorge, que suis-je?'' (p.57). At which point Kyo's question — a sort of reprise of Grabot's — crystallizes the human predicament at yet another level: alienation no longer on the cosmic plane, nor the social and interpersonal, but — just as vital — within the consciousness of the individual human being.

Soon after completing *La Condition humaine* Malraux wrote: 'Ce livre est fondamentalement, pour moi, celui du drame de la conscience' (*62*, p.78). And if the predicament is highlighted in this or that particular case, it has a universal impact. As Malraux would later insist, 'ce qui m'intéresse dans un homme quelconque, c'est la condition humaine' (*3*, p.22). When Kyo is overwhelmed in Hankow by 'l'angoisse de n'être qu'un homme, que lui-même' (p.148), he knows that what he feels extends beyond himself — immediately as 'l'angoisse primordiale' which afflicts Tchen (p.151), but also in accord with his father's belief that 'le fond de l'homme est l'angoisse, la conscience de sa propre fatalité' (ibid.). The feeling is as much bodily as intellectual: its essence is suffering, whether Gisors's with the pain welling up inside him after the death of Kyo (p.314), or Tchen's after the explosion of his bomb, when 'rien n'existait que la douleur' (p.236). Tchen's experience here, in the seconds before his death, confirms in its own way the Christian lesson Smithson had tried to teach him hours earlier: 'Mon pauvre petit [...] chacun de nous ne connaît que sa propre douleur' (p.167). Smithson is unwittingly paraphrasing Kyo, discussing Clappique earlier: 'Tout homme ressemble à sa douleur' (p.46). That discussion

proves inconclusive, but Kyo's aphorism clearly has the widest
application. Beginning with his own situation in the aftermath of
May's infidelity and the shock of hearing his own voice, he struggles
to come to terms with the precise nature of suffering, and finally
realises that it lies at the very core of human identity: the 'monstre
incomparable, préférable à tout, que tout être est pour soi-même et
qu'il choie dans son cœur' (p.57). In the depths of the self, as in the
vastness of space and the complexity of the social world, the human
condition can only be a state of separation.

**************

### 'Modes de vie'

Malraux is acutely aware of both the responsibilities and the
constraints facing the modern novelist. As he sees it, the task of any
artistic creator is to avoid one-sided sermonizing. 'Ce n'est pas la
passion qui détruit l'œuvre d'art', he writes in the preface to *Le
Temps du mépris*, 'c'est la volonté de prouver.' The value of the
work, he continues, derives from the harmony it achieves: 'l'accord
entre ce qu'elle exprime et les moyens qu'elle emploie' (*1*, p.776).
At the same time, the contemporary moral and intellectual climate
has a pervasive influence. 'Je crois,' declared Malraux in 1929,

> que, depuis que la chrétienté a disparu en tant
> qu'armature du monde, le romancier, après le
> philosophe, est devenu un homme qui propose — qu'on
> le veuille ou non — un certain nombre de modes de vie.
> (*1*, p.287)

The differences between a novel such as *La Condition humaine* and a
polemic such as Pascal's *Apologie* need little further emphasis. The
dynamic narrative of Malraux's text could scarcely promote a
consistent doctrine as the *Pensées* do. And if both authors favour the
dialogue form, Pascal exploits it systematically to demolish argu-
ments against Christian belief, whereas for Malraux it is a way of
allowing contrasting attitudes to coexist. Further, Malraux's use of

multiple narrative viewpoints, together with the restrictions on the 'omniscient' or extradiegetic narrator, excludes the possibility of any single 'line' being privileged above others. However rich *La Condition humaine* may be in ideas and systems of belief, none can be detached from the novelistic context.

The various 'modes de vie' are presented more or less explicitly as ways in which characters react to their circumstances. The metaphors of captivity, for instance, are consistently counter-balanced by motifs of escape and liberation. Tchen, imprisoned in the world of murder, seeks to be 'délivré' (pp.10, 13, 17); and the same term is used for Gisors, confined within his terrifying solitude (p.71). In another lexical pattern Ferral seeks to *compensate* for Valérie's humiliation of him in the hall of the Astor (p.215), while Hemmelrich's urge to assert himself draws on exactly the same vocabulary: 'Compenser [...] cette vie atroce qui l'empoisonnait depuis qu'il était né'. As Hemmelrich broods on his past, the motif reveals another facet. Why, he asks himself, was he gassed during the Great War? For his country? Hardly: 'Il n'était pas Belge, il était misérable'. Such indeed is the tenor of his whole life: 'D'un bout à l'autre, il n'était que misère' (p.180). Albeit unwittingly, Hemmelrich provides his own version of Pascal's fundamental image of man without God: of 'misère', poverty, destitution at once material, moral and cosmic.

'Que faire d'une âme s'il n'y a ni Dieu, ni Christ?'(p.67): Gisors's question clearly has a general application, excluding as it does the hypothesis of the Pascalian 'félicité de l'homme avec Dieu'. Christianity nevertheless remains a frequent presence in the text — a 'mode de vie' to be taken into account. Ferral, in his relationship with the apparently shameless Valérie, hopes to trade off 'la honte chrétienne, la reconnaissance pour la honte subie' (p.120), the streets of Hankow contain 'silhouettes de purgatoire' (p.147), and when the lost cyanide capsule is recovered Katow's relief comes out — ironically enough — in the words 'O résurrection!' (p.308). But the residual significance of Christianity is most fully expressed through the evolution of Tchen, an orphan acquiring both Augustinian and Lutheran ideas before turning to political activism under Gisors's influence at the University of Peking. If he ultimately rejects the submissiveness he sees in Christianity, his chance meeting with Pastor Smithson, his former teacher, reveals his continuing respect: 'Cet homme parlait de lui-même et disait la vérité. Comme lui, celui-là vivait sa pensée; il était autre chose qu'une loque avide' (p.168). Even having abandoned any trace of Christian faith Tchen retains essentially religious instincts: a capacity for mysticism (p.151), and an aspiration to ecstasy (p.150) — which will be realized in his last moments, when he runs towards Chiang's car 'avec une joie d'extatique' (p.235).

Tchen is one of a number of figures who openly recognize the necessity of a principle to live by. Reflecting on Vologuine in Hankow, he accepts that, whatever their differences, 'quand on vit comme nous, il faut une certitude [...]. Il faut que quelque chose soit sûr' (pp.148–49). And Clappique understands how most people function — albeit admitting that he is exceptional in escaping 'presque tout sur quoi les hommes fondent leur vie: amour, famille, travail' (p.257). Kyo, for his part, has constructed a notional framework of fundamental values: 'christianisme pour l'esclavage, nation pour le citoyen, communisme pour l'ouvrier' (p.228). And it is from this starting point that Gisors, in his dialogue with Ferral, articulates his own personal theory. While reluctant to discuss his son's thinking with Ferral, Gisors puts forward a schematic set of strategies adopted by different cultures 'pour s'affranchir' — opium in China, hashish in Islamic countries, sex for Westerners. And where Tchen had simply asserted: 'Il faut une certitude', Gisors, echoing Baudelaire, insists: 'Il faut toujours s'intoxiquer'. The image hardly comes as a surprise, given both local custom and Gisors's inclination to associate others' escape attempts with his own. Nevertheless its implications reach deep into the text. Clappique, he later says, will not grow old, because 'l'âge ne le menait pas à l'expérience humaine mais à l'intoxication [...] où se conjugueraient enfin tous ses moyens d'ignorer la vie' (p.263). Clappique, in his turn, witnessing the bloodlust with which König keeps reality at bay, is stunned by 'cette intoxication totale, que le sang seul assouvissait' (p.268), and König himself makes the specific comparison with

opium smokers (p.267). If the primary object of intoxication is to
distract from the intolerable circumstances of existence, the nature of
the experience will nevertheless vary enormously as between, say,
the elimination of pain on the one hand and the reordering of
perception on the other. While Gisors chooses not to pursue this line
in detail, he nevertheless conveys something of the range of the
novel's 'modes de vie' — compulsions, beliefs, values, ideologies.
'Tchen et le meurtre, Clappique et sa folie, Katow et la révolution,
May et l'amour, lui-même et l'opium...' (p.228): the suspension
points suggest strongly that the list could be continued, even if
Gisors finds no 'drug' with which to identify Kyo, the son he
manifestly idealizes. In any case this 'contre-courant confus et caché
de figures' — unspoken, incomplete and firmly identified with
individuals — flows from one personal perspective, however well
informed: it is certainly not a systematic overview, let alone an
authoritative judgement. Taken along with others' more fragmentary
perceptions, however, it offers a practical basis for a fuller scrutiny
and a more balanced, less personalized reading of the issues it raises.

    As Gisors's off-the-cuff thoughts make clear, opium is a
conveniently literal addiction. The frantic taxi-driver Kyo and Katow
find 'en état de besoin' (p.42) is one of many thousands; Tchen and
(reputedly) Ferral are familiar with opium (pp.150, 321); and Gisors
has been addicted for twenty years: 'On lui prêtait la patience des
bouddhistes: c'était celle des intoxiqués' (p.45). He will successively
rely on it as his only chance to escape the solitude which haunts him
(pp.71–72, 262), abandon it when forced to confront the world after
Kyo's death (pp.313–14), then return to it when exiled in Japan, in
an ultimate denial of the claims of reality: 'Il faudrait que les
hommes pussent savoir qu'il n'y a pas de réel, qu'il est des mondes
de contemplation — avec ou sans opium — où tout est vain' (p.333).
Clappique, too, uses the drug (p.246), and Gisors considers him
ideally suited to it (p.46) — but Clappique, along with others
(Tchen's companion in the lift, p.15; Kama's drunken servant,
p.191), prefers alcohol. This is what sustains the 'farfelu' world of
his imagining: the fantasies of the *Black Cat* or the brothel, the antics
in his hotel room, and his improvisation on the ship leaving

Shanghai, culminating in: 'Allons nous saouler' (p.296). Clappique's 'folie' reveals psychological rather than physical dependence. In Gisors's view 'sa mythomanie est un moyen de nier la vie [...]. Rien n'existe: tout est rêve' (p.45). And if his fantasizing works primarily by eliminating harsh reality from his consciousness ('il ne vivait plus que dans l'univers romanesque qu'il venait de créer', p.247), it also serves to attenuate his own substance. When he describes himself as 'le seul homme de Shanghaï qui n'existe pas' (p.195), the self-mockery cannot hide the pathos.

'Peut-être l'amour est-il surtout le moyen qu'emploie l'Occidental pour s'affranchir de sa condition d'homme' (p.228): Gisors's speculation is anticipated by Valérie, who identifies sexual adventure as an escape in her elegant aphorism: 'Les hommes ont des voyages, les femmes ont des amants' (p.117) — which might well apply to May, given her episode with Lenglen. But Gisors must be thinking especially of his interlocutor, Ferral. Once again, 'amour' has an essentially physical connotation. Soon Ferral will be bitterly reflecting:

> Peut-être avait-il aimé, autrefois. Autrefois. Quel psychologue ivre mort avait inventé d'appeler amour le sentiment qui maintenant empoisonnait sa vie? [...] Les femmes l'obsédaient [...] comme un désir de vengeance. [...]. Condamné aux coquettes ou aux putains. Il y avait les corps. (pp.230–31)

For Ferral sex provides a way out of his own insignificance through the domination of another: in his brutal formula, 'l'homme peut et doit nier la femme' (p.228). This is his attitude to Valérie, whom he seeks to reduce to a mere object ('un corps conquis avait d'avance pour lui plus de goût qu'un corps livré', pp.214), and likewise to the Chinese courtesan, to be subjugated through 'érotisme' (p.232). But Ferral's addictive need to dominate finds other outlets too. Martial is among many colleagues who prove the point: 'Il avait un talent unique pour leur refuser l'existence' (p.83). In public as in private his objective — his release — is nothing less than 'la possession des moyens de contraindre les choses ou les hommes' (p.226), and his ultimate value the individualistic 'efficacité' of the buccaneering capitalist.

Ferral's addiction can be interpreted as a mild version of the fascist König's urge to destroy his victims — an antidote to his own past humiliation as a prisoner in Siberia (p.266). But the compulsion to kill is not restricted to a single political outlook or mental disposition, and can be far more complex than in König's case. It is because Tchen has turned from puritanical Christianity to Marxism that he kills the arms dealer, but as a result of this defining experience, the means of revolution become an end in themselves. The late-night conversation with Gisors reveals how much Tchen has changed: 'Gisors était épouvanté par cette sensation soudaine, cette certitude [...] d'une intoxication aussi terrible que la sienne l'était peu' (p.65). Terrorism is a 'fascination' (p.63), and destruction the only activity with which Tchen can identify (p.143). But if Tchen is an extreme case — a loner, by definition falling outside normal parameters, he is still one element of the Marxist-Leninist revolutionary movements of the 1920s. His position on the edge of the ideological spectrum becomes clearer in the debate with his accomplices. Where Tchen sees his actions as part of a solipsistic cult in which he will sacrifice himself ('Pas une religion [...]. La possession complète de soi-même', p.185), Peï wants communism to revive the Chinese nation and rid it of imperialists, while Souen brings it to bear on the interests of the poor (pp.182–83). Debates elsewhere highlight more shades of opinion — other 'modes de vie' — within the Communist camp. The lengthy dialogues with Vologuine and Possoz in Hankow bring out the cautious pragmatism of the Comintern, requiring continued compromise with Chiang, as against the Shanghai communists' straightforward aim of sustaining the impetus of their uprising. Even Katow, remembering Lenin's tactics during the civil war in Russia, accepts the need to keep the support of the Kuomintang, at least until the initial military and political gains are secured (p.127). Katow, however, manifestly lives and dies for the principles of Communist revolution rather than abiding by expedients. His exemplary commitment to the cause is such that after the abortive action in Odessa he had volunteered to accompany less privileged prisoners to the lead mines (pp.40, 127, 209); and in Kyo's view he would do the same again: 'Il irait pour l'idée qu'il a de la vie, de lui-même' (p.53). Kyo, too, shows unquestionable devotion to the revolutionary movement. He identifies unequivocally with the dispossessed — in the Chinese context, the rural peasantry and the urban working class (pp.68–69); his organisational skills make him, even more than Katow, indispensable to the success of the uprising (p.43); and ideologically, while relatively independent of Hankow and Moscow, he maintains a consistent Marxist line. At the same time, Kyo's values extend beyond the strictly political, for at their heart lies a distinguishing belief in the intrinsic worth of all human beings, to be defended at all costs. His aim is to give to each oppressed individual 'la possession de sa propre dignité' (p.68), as is understood by both Gisors (ibid.) and Clappique (p.265). And it is precisely in upholding this principle against the sadistic König, and refusing any humiliating trade-off, that Kyo consigns himself to death (pp.286–90).

'Les questions individuelles ne se posaient pour Kyo que dans sa vie privée' (p.68). But whereas the personal lives of the other revolutionaries are relegated to the background, Kyo's assumes particular prominence, and takes the scrutiny of 'modes de vie' on to a different plane. If the initial glimpse into his marriage shows up May's infidelity, which casts a persistent shadow, the couple remain united in 'la plus étroite complicité' (p.57) — a lexical counter to the motifs of separation. With all its imperfections, their relationship offers a unique consolation:

> 'Avec elle seule j'ai en commun cet amour déchiré ou non [...].' Ce n'était certes pas le bonheur, c'était quelque chose de primitif qui s'accordait aux ténèbres [...] — la seule chose en lui qui fût aussi forte que la mort. (p.58)

It is of course with May that Gisors identifies the values of 'l'amour' (and here 'love' must be the sense), and he later recognizes that the love of Kyo is his only real point of contact with her (p.333). The rare 'complicité' binding her to Kyo stems from an intuitive and uncritical acceptance of a whole person rather than any calculated judgement: 'Pour May seule, il n'était pas ce qu'il avait fait; pour lui seul, elle était toute autre chose que sa biographie' (p.57). The resolution of their disagreement just before Kyo's arrest is unconditional: 'Accepter d'entraîner l'être qu'on aime dans la mort est peut-être la forme totale de l'amour, celle qui ne peut pas être dépassée' (p.204). Even death itself cannot undo the complicity. Tending Kyo's body, ''mon amour,' murmurait-elle, comme elle eût dit 'ma chair', sachant bien que c'était quelque chose d'elle-même, non d'étranger, qui lui était arraché; 'ma vie ...'' (p.311).

In a more summary way, Kama represents the same principle, explaining that he paints out of love for his wife (p.189). Even if he does not figure in Gisors's improvised list, Kama occupies a vital place in the text precisely because his values are so different from those of most other characters. As their discussion unfolds, Clappique feels ill at ease in the presence of 'un être qui nie la douleur' (p.191) — who disregards what is, for most, the fundamental experience. Similarly for Gisors, by the end 'le vieux peintre appartenait à un autre univers' (p.192). What sets Kama apart is his Oriental conception of painting. Whereas Western painters express their own individuality, he sees painting as a way of merging with the world: 'Pour moi, c'est le monde qui compte', or, more emphatically: 'Aller du signe à la chose signifiée, c'est approfondir le monde' (p.190). But even Kama, for all the ethereal serenity he seems to personify, requires his own means of escape. Driven by Gisors's persistent questioning to imagine the death of his wife, Kama literally withdraws from the conversation. Gisors explains that he is playing the traditional stringed instrument known as the shamisen: 'Toujours, lorsque quelque chose l'a troublé: hors du Japon, c'est sa défense... Il m'a dit, en revenant d'Europe: 'je sais maintenant que je peux retrouver n'importe où mon silence intérieur...'' (p.192). Gisors's list could have ended with 'Kama et la musique'.

*Evaluations*

Malraux's 'human condition' does not lend itself to clear-cut
remedies. Even Kyo's values — which might be thought more valid
than most — are suggested by negatives as much as stated positively:
the love of May means that for her he is *not* merely the sum of his
acts (p.57); and he explains 'la dignité humaine' as 'le contraire de
l'humiliation' (p.288). At the same time the design of the text
consistently leaves space for evaluation, even in the early stages and
increasingly as time passes, notably in the summative dialogue
between Gisors and Ferral, and in the final conversation in Kobe.
There is, too, a recurrent emphasis on the learning processes through
which the main characters pass, for their ideas can and do evolve
over time. Tchen, thinking back to his discussion with Gisors,
suddenly grasps the essence of terrorist action (p.185); Kyo, making
peace with May, can finally comprehend what their relationship has
meant (p.204); and the same vocabulary renders Clappique's flash of
understanding at the roulette table: 'Il comprenait maintenant la vie
intense des instruments de jeu' (p.242). Another lexical pattern
reflects a common need to give sense and direction to existence.
Thus Kama, wondering if he could communicate with his wife even
after death, reasons: 'C'est le plus difficile, mais peut-être est-ce le
sens de la vie' (p.192). Others are forced to face the loss of any such
coherence. For Gisors, after Kyo's death 'le monde n'avait plus de
sens' (p.314), while in Ferral's eyes 'tous les événements de
Shanghaï allaient se dissoudre là dans un non-sens total' (p.327).
More devastating yet is the growth of self-awareness, typically
revealing the extent of personal failure. Spurned by Valérie and
trying to compensate by degrading the courtesan, Ferral reaches a
damning verdict on himself: 'Il comprenait maintenant […]. Il
posséderait à travers cette Chinoise qui l'attendait, la seule chose
dont il fût avide: lui-même' (p.232). On the wall the Tibetan painting
of the embracing skeletons is an unforgiving parallel. König, having
failed to bring Kyo under his control, reflects bleakly on his
interrogation of a former member of the Soviet police: 'Deux heures
plus tôt, il avait interrogé un tchékiste prisonnier; après dix minutes il
l'avait senti fraternel. Leur monde, à tous deux, n'était plus celui des

hommes' (pp.289–90). At the other end of the political scale Tchen
learns that, living purely for the violence of revolution, he can have
no place in the Communist future his comrades anticipate: 'Le
monde qu'ils préparaient ensemble le condamnait, lui, Tchen, autant
que celui de leurs ennemis. Que ferait-il dans l'usine future
embusqué derrière leurs cottes bleues?' (p.102; see also May's
comment on Tchen, p.334).

Certain individuals submit entirely to collective authority —
the sanctimonious Vologuine on the Left, the pusillanimous Parisian
financiers on the Right. But this is an immediate expediency which
excludes any personal statement: a refusal even to enter the forum
where the novel's human issues are tested out. Clappique, at least,
does make individual choices, even if they demonstrate only that he
cannot take responsibility for any life — his own included. Though
capable of saving Kyo from arrest, he loses himself in roulette
(gambling, of course, being as pervasive a 'mode de vie' as opium in
Shanghai). In one imaginative leap the game becomes the apotheosis
of Clappique's 'folie', and its own absurd justification: 'Il lui sembla
soudain que la banque lui devait de l'argent non parce qu'il avait
misé sur le numéro gagnant [...]; mais de toute éternité, à cause de la
fantaisie et de la liberté de son esprit' (p.240). Beyond Clappique's
rejection of any meaningful role in a real world, this scene yields
another sort of symbolism. For in Clappique's increasingly
extravagant thoughts 'cette boule dont le mouvement allait faiblir
était un destin, et d'abord *son* destin' (p.241). According to this
bizarre logic, material gain is meaning-less and what counts is the
impression Clappique has of determining his own fate: 'Qu'avait à
voir avec l'argent cette boule [...] par quoi il étreignait son propre
destin, le seul moyen qu'il eût jamais trouvé de se posséder lui-
même!' (pp.241–42). The ultimate irony, though, has emerged
earlier, when Clappique deluded himself into thinking that he was
defining his very being through the act of gambling: 'C'était dans
cette salle que le sang affluait à la vie. Ceux qui ne jouaient pas
n'étaient pas des hommes' (p.241). Eventually Gisors will make his
own judgement: '[Clappique] pouvait cesser d'exister, disparaître
dans un vice, dans une monomanie, il ne pouvait devenir un homme'

(p.263). But if Clappique's posture is all too absurd, the notion of implacable forces bearing down on the individual can be taken seriously. The imagery applied to Ferral's business operations makes an unambiguous link: 'Il se souvint avec orgueil du mot d'un de ses adversaires: ''Ferral veut toujours qu'une banque soit une maison de jeu'' (p.328). Ferral, too, consciously risks his own resources in a game of chance preordained by fate; and although the Consortium has been successful, his position becomes precarious as soon as his American credits are withdrawn (p.212): 'Ses cartes ne pouvaient toutes gagner pendant une période de crise chinoise aiguë' (p.214). Ferral is up against not the random movements of the roulette wheel, nor even the law of averages, but 'ces poussées de l'économie mondiale' (ibid.): what Kyo elsewhere calls the 'fatalités économiques' (p.145) play the role of destiny in this post-Christian universe. Regardless of his politics or psychology — perhaps even because of them — Ferral's career is an increasingly precarious wager. This is clearly signalled at the moment of his downfall, when he realizes the extent of his vulnerability: 'Cette nuit, que ce fût dans la résistance, la victoire ou la défaite, il se sentait dépendant de toutes les forces du monde' (p.214). The echo of Kyo, uncertainly contemplating the imminent uprising, is hardly fortuitous: 'Il n'était plus qu'inquiétude et attente. […]. Victoire ou défaite, le destin du monde, cette nuit, hésitait près d'ici' (pp.47–48). At which point political differences recede, giving place to deeper thematic patterns. At stake here is not time-bound ideology but the unending struggle of human beings against whatever implacable forces threaten to oppress, constrain and destroy them.

Kyo's Communist credentials, acquired over years of patient effort (pp.67–69), parallel the record of the president of the Consortium (pp.85, 89), just as his Marxist analysis of the world revolutionary movement (pp.147–48) has its counterpart in Ferral's assessment of international trade (pp.212–14). And in each case intellectual understanding is informed by ethical principle: the defence of human dignity on one hand, and the assertion of human will on the other. But the status of both Kyo and Ferral is finally determined in another way. Through the decisive sequence in Paris when he is denied support, Ferral is forced to accept the dissolution of his commercial operation: 'Il était battu; ayant fait de l'efficacité sa valeur essentielle, rien ne compensait qu'il se trouvât en face de ces hommes [...] dans cette position humiliée' (p.326). But as the one individual distinguishable from the effete, caramel-sucking representatives of a fearful conservative establishment, Ferral leaves the text with his human stature enhanced. Gisors's lesson to his students is a fitting epitaph: 'Le capitalisme moderne. [...] est beaucoup plus volonté d'organisation que de puissance' (p.230). Kyo's trajectory is a clearer instance of triumph in the face of ostensible defeat. If his uprising is ruthlessly crushed, and its leaders killed or dispersed, the conviction remains that its momentum will continue: 'La Révolution venait de passer par une terrible maladie, mais elle n'était pas morte. Et c'était Kyo et les siens, vivants ou non, vaincus ou non, qui l'avaient mise au monde' (p.330. This is an ironic reworking of the metaphor with which Vologuine defended the Comintern's tactics: 'Il s'agit de l'accoucher [la Révolution]. Et pas de la faire avorter' (p.139). The setback is merely temporary: the project is not doomed. But more important in terms of the text, Kyo — even more evidently than Ferral — resists all the forces of fate, however defined. He departs from Party orthodoxy precisely where it leads to 'l'obsession des fatalités économiques' (p.145). For Kyo, still true to his father's earlier beliefs, 'il y a dans le marxisme le sens d'une fatalité, et l'exaltation d'une volonté. Chaque fois que la fatalité passe avant la volonté, je me méfie' (p.139). The final image of Kyo, choosing death among his own people in the *préau,* is crucial to his ultimate standing. 'Il mourrait', he decides, recalling the idea Gisors had earlier borrowed from him, 'pour avoir donné un sens à la vie. Qu'eût valu une vie pour laquelle il n'eût pas accepté de mourir?' Acutely aware of 'la fatalité acceptée par eux', he defiantly takes his cyanide in a gesture summing up all that precedes it: 'Mourir pouvait être un acte exalté, la suprême expression d'une vie à quoi cette mort ressemblait tant' (p.304). But if Kyo's death, like his life, runs its course on his terms, Katow actually enhances his prestige by the sacrificial manner of his dying — just as his departing shadow is spectacularly magnified. By giving away his cyanide to two terrified comrades he makes 'le plus grand don qu'il eût jamais fait' (p.308). In its deliberate and complete consistency with the principles by which he has lived, Katow's is perhaps the supreme moral victory over fate.

The later stages of the narrative convey a swift succession of climactic events — Tchen's death, Clappique at the casino, the prison scenes, then Ferral at the Ministry of Finance. But the epilogue, set in Japan a year after the insurrection, opens up a fresh angle of vision and invites a re-reading of what has gone before. It offers not only a retrospect of Shanghai in 1927 but a connecting thread to the present — and future — of the survivors. Peï's letter communicates the idealistic view of a workers' state, and reports on a Hemmelrich who now, in Soviet Russia, has found a genuine sense of purpose (pp.329–30). Crucially, however, the denouement is left in the hands of May and Gisors. May has 'kept the faith' in two senses. Her commitment remains intact: she plans to work as a Communist agitator, or, failing that, as a doctor in Siberia. Moreover her love for Kyo has survived, and her sustained political motivation derives from the desire to avenge him (p.331). By contrast Gisors has disengaged almost totally, rejecting the chance to teach in Moscow, denying Kyo's belief in Marxism as a 'volonté' and retreating into passive, opium-induced contemplation (pp.332–33). Gisors has however learned from Kama the value of music as a means of coping with the thought of death. Like the earlier key dialogues in the novel this one also lends weight to both sides of the argument rather than ending in a simplistic endorsement of either. Activism is set against resignation, commitment against detachment, hope for a possible future against nostalgia for a vanished past. Love can — perhaps — resist the rigours of life, and art may be an authentic consolation. 'Tout homme est fou', reflects Gisors, 'mais qu'est une destinée humaine sinon une vie d'efforts pour unir ce fou et l'univers...' (p.335). The problem of human destiny — the interface of self and cosmos — remains stubbornly outside the limits of any unambiguous resolution.

\*\*\*\*\*\*\*\*\*\*\*\*\*\*

*La Condition humaine* is the site of countless tensions: an arena for
debates and conflicts which find expression both technically and in
terms of ideas. It embraces the interplay of light and dark, sound and
silence, action and reflection, and juxtaposes Left and Right, male
and female, youth and age. At different levels lie cross-currents
connecting the most disparate of elements — linguistic registers,
narrative devices, abstract concepts — all contributing to the range
and depth befitting Malraux's ambitious title and cosmopolitan
setting. But the novel's diversity suggests itself in another equally
important way. When Malraux puts aphorisms in the mouths of his
characters, or exploits the mechanics of dialogue, the effect is clearly
to enrich the novel from within. But towards the end it seems
repeatedly as if the text is reaching out beyond conventional
novelistic limits towards other, more august literary forms. Outside
the conversation between Gisors and May, the Kobe sequence
conveys a sense of expansion quite uncharacteristic of the foregoing
narrative — and accentuated by comparison with the pettifogging
dealings in Paris just beforehand. All the emphasis in the scene-
setting falls not, as so often, on the enclosed space of a room, but the
immensity of the sunlit bay beyond. Instead of the pressure of the
usual tight chronology moreover, Gisors feels the wind blowing in
'comme un fleuve, comme le Temps même' (p.335), while the
coolies on the hillside labour with 'le geste millénaire des esclaves'
(p.333). The workers on the road are merely 'des hommes
minuscules' (p.335), whose discordant movements Gisors contrasts
with the 'ruée cosmique' of the animal kingdom (pp.335–36). The
scale is altogether different from that of the rest of the text: the
quotidian dimensions of the novel are straining towards the
timelessness of some ancient epic. Elsewhere there are more explicit
associations. Immediately after Clappique's grotesque byplay —
again juxtaposition heightens the effect — the anguished cries of the
Communist prisoners make up an elegy bestowing on Kyo, stretched
out as in death, 'une majesté de chant funèbre' (p.304). The next day,
when Kyo's body is returned, the routine ambience of the novel
gives way to one of far greater solemnity as Gisors discovers the
depth of his suffering,

> comme si cette contemplation épouvantée eût été la seule
> voix que pût entendre la mort, comme si cette souffrance
> d'être homme dont il s'imprégnait jusqu'au fond du
> cœur eût été la seule oraison que pût entendre le corps de
> son fils tué. (p.314)

Kyo had, indeed, anticipated how his reputation might grow in the future, if his story were to be recast as the life of a martyred saint: 'légende sanglante dont se font les légendes dorées!' (p.304). (By ironic contrast Lou-You-Shen's dramatic recitation fails miserably: 'La vieille communauté chinoise était bien détruite: nul ne l'écoutait' (p.302).)

The most telling association of all occurs when Tchen, preparing his suicide attack on Chiang Kai-Shek, elevates his banal urban setting to another plane of existence. The mist-shrouded passers-by are suddenly assigned to a less time-bound, more grandiose order:

> N'était-ce pas le Destin même, cette force qui les
> poussait vers le fond de l'avenue où l'arc allumé
> d'enseignes à peine visibles devant les ténèbres du
> fleuve semblait les portes mêmes de la mort? (p.234)

Then Tchen looks down the avenue to the signboards covered in Chinese characters which, 'enfoncés en perspectives troubles [...] se perdaient dans ce monde tragique et flou comme dans les siècles' (p.234). Of all the genres *La Condition humaine* assimilates, none is closer in spirit than tragedy, the dramatic form whose essence is to wrest dignity and value from the destruction of flawed humanity. If, for Malraux, the modern novel is not centred on the contingent particularities of the individual, it is 'un moyen d'expression privilégié du tragique de l'homme' (*34*, p.66). The basic scheme is rehearsed in a series of variations: the zealot Tchen in his ecstasy of self-immolation, Kyo affirming his integrity while taking his own life, Katow leaving his comrades as a hero ('toutes les têtes [...] suivaient le rythme de sa marche, avec amour, avec effroi', p.310).

But each death sets up its own confrontation of human value and superhuman destiny; each conveys its own catharsis. In a less elevated — and less final — way the process of promise and defeat is repeated through Gisors, Ferral and Clappique. But in the last analysis the tragic effects are still reconciled with the needs of the novel rather than working against them. There seems a clear invitation to think back to *La Condition humaine* in Malraux's preface to *Le Temps du mépris*: 'Le monde d'une œuvre comme celle-ci, le monde de la tragédie, est toujours le monde antique; l'homme, la foule, les éléments, la femme, le destin.' At the same time, he goes on, tragedy and novel each have their own distinct configurations: '[Ce monde] se réduit à deux personnages, le héros et son sens de la vie; les antagonismes individuels, qui permettent au roman sa complexité, n'y figurent pas' (*1*, p.775). *La Condition humaine* can accommodate the ethos of tragedy — like those of the other forms towards which it gestures — without narrowing its scope. Malraux does not change the nature of the novel, but stretches its limits to the full.

The preface to *Le Temps du mépris* complements the earlier novel in another vital way. Questioning Flaubert's tendency to despise his characters, Malraux puts himself unequivocally in the opposite camp: 'On peut aimer que le sens du mot 'art' soit tenter de donner conscience à des hommes de la grandeur qu'ils ignorent en eux' (1, p.776). There are powerful resonances at work here, for *La Condition humaine* serves this purpose deliberately and openly. As well as enshrining the heroism of Katow, Kyo and others as individuals, the *préau* scene aligns them with their fellow human beings. It is, precisely, Kyo who reflects that 'chacun de ces hommes avait rageusement saisi au passage la seule grandeur qui pût être la sienne' (p.301). And just as specifically, May reminds Gisors of the terms in which he earlier described Kyo, Katow and their comrades: 'ceux qui ont donné conscience de leur révolte à trois cents millions de misérables' (p.332). Ultimately, however, the 'sens du mot 'art'' concerns Malraux the artist. The preoccupation with artistic creation will never leave him, as is endlessly and eloquently proved throughout his work, but one discussion — in *L'Espoir* — stands out. As the fires burn in the streets of Madrid, Scali and Garcia — not unlike Gisors and Ferral at the Shanghai Cercle Français during the fighting — address what they see as ultimate human values. Their exchange deals not with intoxicants or escape-routes but, rather, achievement. To the question: 'Qu'est-ce qu'un homme peut faire de mieux de sa vie?', the answer comes back: 'Transformer en conscience une expérience aussi large que possible' (2, p.337). The formulation is utterly characteristic of an author whose ambition is to expand and deepen his reader's awareness. The aspiration of *La Condition humaine* has surely never been more trenchantly stated.

# 5. READINGS

One of *La Condition humaine*'s first reviewers, Emmanuel Berl, in *Marianne* in May 1933, immediately saw it as a major event: an already significant young novelist articulating nothing less than the spirit of the age. In November, the award of the *prix Goncourt* gained the book far more attention than was usual. And from the outset the range of reactions matched the many-sidedness of the text. There was wholesale denunciation in the Catholic journal *La Croix* ('a depraved Communist novel'), and the more measured reproaches of the political Right ('grandeur, but of an inhuman, barbaric kind' declared Robert Brasillach in *L'Action Française*) and the orthodox Left (for Ilya Ehrenburg in *Izvestia* 'these heroes seem like fanatical romantics'). By complete contrast Trotsky in *La Vérité* hailed a 'devastating indictment' of the Comintern, and the American Edmund Wilson in *New Republic* praised the vivid dramatization of contrasting cultures and moral systems.

As his career and image evolved over the Thirties and Forties, judgments of the novel were inevitably coloured by changing perceptions of Malraux. A special number of *Esprit* in October 1948, for instance, tackled 'le cas Malraux' almost entirely in relation to his controversial political positions. But Frohock's authoritative 1952 study argued resolutely for literary interpretation based on the texts themselves rather than extraneous ideology. The next year brought another essential work in Picon's illuminating *Malraux par lui-même* — truer to its title than other volumes in the same series, since Malraux responded, in marginal notes, to Picon's observations. Rapidly — and thanks as much to *La Condition humaine* as anything else — Malraux became a landmark for all and sundry: a recurrent reference point in the landscape of modern fiction. Alongside the extensive body of specialist criticism which has built up since the 1960s are readings reflecting any number of current trends. In *Pour une sociologie du roman* (1965) Lucien Goldmann applied structuralist perspectives. The feminist Annie Leclerc contrived a simplistically macho target in her *Parole de femme* (1974). Régis Debray, a revolutionary of a younger generation, acclaimed the creator of a 'modern myth' (*André Malraux ou l'impératif du mensonge*, 1977). The list goes on.

Although Malraux once claimed that the world eventually came to resemble his fiction, even he could not have anticipated all the radical changes in the decades since his novel was published: the countless discoveries in the physical universe, all the antagonisms and convulsions in politics, economics and belief systems worldwide, and the shifting perceptions of self and identity — not forgetting the redefinitions of art-forms and the transformations of the literary text. But as he argued in *L'Homme précaire et la littérature*, the time of the author coexists with that of the reader — present and future. The experience of Gide is still exemplary. If his first encounter with *La Condition humaine* left him baffled, on rereading he found it 'ordonné dans la confusion, d'une intelligence admirable et [...] profondément enfoncé dans la vie' (*Journal 1889–1939*, 10 avril 1933). The intervening years have merely confirmed the richness of this ever-engaging text and the unending variety of experience it offers the reader. In a formula so eerily reminiscent of Malraux that critical expression, like the world itself, sometimes seems to take its lead from him, Barthes wrote, 'une œuvre est 'éternelle', non parce qu'elle impose un sens unique à des hommes différents, mais parce qu'elle suggère des sens différents à un homme unique'.[11]

---

[11] Roland Barthes, *Critique et vérité* (Paris, Seuil, 1966), p.51.

## La Condition humaine: a summary

|  | Parts 1, 2 | Part 3 |
|---|---|---|
| **Pages** | 9–78; 79–131 | 133–59 |
| **Time** | 21–22–23 March 1927 | 29 March |
| **Place** | Shanghai | Hankow |
| **Main Events** | Communist strike, then armed uprising. Chiang Kai-Shek approaches. | Discussions at Comintern HQ: no support for Communists in Shanghai. |
| **Characters** | | |
| **Tchen** | 9–20; 59–64; 90–107; 123–31 | 142–52 |
| **Kyo** | 17–37; 41–58; 72–78; 122–31 | 133–59 |
| **Katow** | 17–27; 37–43; 72–78; 126–31 | |
| **Hemmelrich** | 17–23 | |
| **Clappique** | 29–37; 55–56 | |
| **Gisors** | 43–47; 58–72 | |
| **May** | 48–56 | |
| **Ferral** | 79–90; 107–22 | |
| **Valérie** | 117–22 | |
| **Vologuine** | | 136–47 |
| **Possoz** | | 152–58 |
| **Peï** | | |
| **Souen** | | |
| **König** | | |

| *Parts 4, 5, 6* | *Part 7* |
|---|---|
| 161–236; 237–77; 279-314 | 315–38 |
| 11–12–13 April | July 1927<br>Spring 1928 |
| Shanghai | Paris<br>Kobe |
| Chiang Kai-Shek overcomes Communists, whose leaders are captured and executed. | Negotiations at Ministry of Finance. Final conversation of survivors. |
|  |  |
| 165–79; 182–87; 233–36 |  |
| 193–205; 248–51; 279–90; 300–09 |  |
| 203–10; 256–57; 269–73; 296–310 |  |
| 177–82; 205–10; 252–57; 269–77 |  |
| 161–65; 187–96; 237–48;<br>257–69; 290–96 |  |
| 187–92; 195–99; 223–30;<br>259–63; 311–14 | 331–38 |
| 195–205; 248–52; 311–13 | 329–38 |
| 211–33 | 315–29 |
|  |  |
|  |  |
|  |  |
| 169–79; 182–87 |  |
| 169–79; 182–87; 270–73; 305–09 |  |
| 264–69; 286–90 |  |

# Select Bibliography

For more complete bibliographical information on Malraux, see John B. Romeiser, *André Malraux: A Reference Guide 1940–1990* (New York, G. K. Hall and Co., 1994). There are regular updates in *Revue André Malraux Review*.

## SELECTED WORKS BY MALRAUX

1. Malraux, André, *Œuvres complètes*, I (Paris, Gallimard, Bibliothèque de la Pléiade, 1989) [includes *Lunes en papier, Ecrit pour une idole à trompe, La Tentation de l'Occident, Les Conquérants, Royaume-Farfelu, La Voie royale, La Condition humaine, Le Temps du mépris*].
2. ——, *Œuvres complètes*, II (Paris, Gallimard, Bibliothèque de la Pléiade, 1996) [includes *L'Espoir, Les Noyers de l'Altenburg, Le Démon de l'absolu*].
3. ——, *Œuvres complètes*, III (Paris, Gallimard, Bibliothèque de la Pléiade, 1996) [includes *Le Miroir des limbes (I. Antimémoires:II. La Corde et les Souris), Oraisons funèbres, Le Règne du Malin*].
4. 'D'une jeunesse européenne', *Ecrits* (*Les Cahiers Verts*, LXX) (Paris, Grasset, 1927), pp.129–53.
5. *L'Homme précaire et la littérature* (Paris, Gallimard, 1977).
6. 'Néocritique', in *Malraux: Etre et dire*, ed. Martine Courcel (Paris, Plon, 1976), pp.295–337.
7. *Scènes choisies* (Paris, Gallimard, 1946).
8. *Les Voix du silence* (Paris, Gallimard, 1951).

## GENERAL STUDIES

9. *André Malraux*, ed.Harold Bloom (New York, New Haven and Philadelphia, Chelsea House, 1988).
10. *André Malraux: Unité de l'œuvre, unité de l'homme*, ed. Christiane Moatti and David Bevan (Paris, La Documentation Française, 1989).
11. Biet, Christian, Jean-Paul Brighelli and Jean-Luc Rispail, *André Malraux: la création d'un destin* (Paris, Gallimard, Découvertes, 1987).
12. Blend, Charles D., *André Malraux, Tragic Humanist* (Columbus, Ohio State University Press, 1963).
13. Boak, Denis, *André Malraux* (Oxford University Press, 1968).
14. Carduner, Jean, *La Création romanesque chez Malraux* (Paris, Nizet, 1968).

15. Cate, Curtis, *André Malraux: A Biography* (London, Hutchinson, 1995).
16. Côté, Paul Raymond, *Les Techniques picturales chez Malraux: interrogation et métamorphose* (Sherbrooke, Editions Naaman, 1984).
17. Dorenlot, Françoise, *Malraux ou l'unité de pensée* (Paris, Gallimard, 1970).
18. Fitch, Brian, *Les Deux Univers romanesques d'André Malraux* (Paris, Lettres Modernes, 1964).
19. Frohock, W. M., *André Malraux and the Tragic Imagination* (Stanford University Press, 1952).
20. Gaillard, Pol, *Les Critiques de notre temps et Malraux* (Paris, Garnier, 1970).
21. Godard, Henri, *L'Autre Face de la littérature. Essai sur André Malraux et la littérature* (Paris, Gallimard, 1990).
22. Greshoff, C. J., *An Introduction to the Novels of André Malraux* (Cape Town and Rotterdam, A. A. Balkema, 1975).
23. Harris, Geoffrey, *André Malraux: l'éthique comme fonction de l'esthétique* (Paris, Lettres Modernes, 1972).
24. ——, *De l'Indochine au RPF, une continuité politique: les romans d'André Malraux* (Toronto, Paratexte, 1990).
25. ——, *André Malraux: A Reassessment* (Basingstoke and London, Macmillan, 1996).
26. Hartman, Geoffrey, H., *Malraux* (London, Bowes and Bowes, 1960).
27. Hoffmann, Joseph, *L'Humanisme de Malraux* (Paris, Klincksieck, 1963).
28. Lacouture, Jean, *Malraux, une vie dans le siècle, 1901–1976* (Paris, Seuil, 1976).
29. Langlois, Walter,*Via Malraux: Essays by Walter Langlois*, collected by David Bevan (Wolfville, The Malraux Society, 1986).
30. Madsen, Axel, *Malraux: A Biography* (New York, William Morrow, 1976).
31. *Malraux: A Collection of Critical Essays*, ed. R.W.B. Lewis (Englewood Cliffs, Prentice-Hall, 1964).
32. Moatti, Christiane, *Le Prédicateur et ses masques: les personnages d'André Malraux* (Paris, Publications de la Sorbonne, 1987).
33. Payne, Robert, *A Portrait of André Malraux* (Englewood Cliffs, Prentice-Hall, 1970).
34. Picon, Gaëtan, *Malraux par lui-même* (Paris, Seuil, 1953).
35. Raymond, Gino, *André Malraux: Politics and the Temptation of Myth* (Aldershot, Avebury, 1995).
36. Saint-Cheron, François de, *L'Esthétique de Malraux* (Paris, SEDES, 1996).
37. Stéphane, Roger, *André Malraux: entretiens et précisions* (Paris, Gallimard, 1984).

*38.*  Suarès, Guy, *Malraux, celui qui vient* (Paris, Stock, 1974).
*39.*  Tarica, Ralph, *Imagery in the Novels of André Malraux* (Cranbury, London and Toronto, Associated University Press, 1980).
*40.*  Tison-Braun, Micheline, *Ce monstre incomparable: Malraux ou l'énigme du moi* (Paris, Armand Colin, 1983).
*41.*  *Witnessing André Malraux: Visions and Re-visions*, ed. Brian Thompson and Carl A. Viggiani (Middleton, Wesleyan University Press, 1984).


*SPECIAL ISSUES ON MALRAUX*


*42.*  *Esprit*, VI, 149 (October 1948).
*43.*  *Europe*, 727–28 (November–December 1989).
*44.*  *L'Herne*, 43 (1982).
*45.*  *Magazine Littéraire*, 79–80 (1973).
*46.*  *Magazine Littéraire*, 347 (1996).
*47.*  *New York Literary Forum*, 3 (1979).
*48.*  *La Nouvelle Revue Française*, 295 (1977).
*49.*  *La Nouvelle Revue Française*, 526 (1996).
*50.*  *Revue d'Histoire Littéraire de la France*, LXXXI, 2 (1981).
*51.*  *Twentieth-Century Literature*, XXIV, 3 (1978).
*52.*  *Yale French Studies*, 18 (1957).


*The following periodicals are devoted to the work of Malraux:*


*André Malraux* (Paris, *La Revue des Lettres Modernes*, 1972– ).
*Mélanges Malraux Miscellany* (Laramie, 1969–83; Edmonton, 1983-86).
*Revue André Malraux Review* (Edmonton, 1986–96; Knoxville, 1996– )


*STUDIES OF LA CONDITION HUMAINE*


*53.*  *André Malraux's 'Man's Fate'*, ed. Harold Bloom (New York, New Haven and Philadelphia, Chelsea House, 1988).
*54.*  Bréchon, Robert, '*La Condition humaine' d'André Malraux* (Paris, Hachette, 1972).
*55.*  Broyer, Jean, *Malraux: 'La Condition humaine'* (Paris, Ellipses, 1996).
*56.*  *'La Condition humaine': roman de l'anti-destin*, ed. Jean-Claude Larrat (Orléans, Paradigme, 1995).
*57.*  Cornud-Peyron, Mireille, *'La Condition humaine' de Malraux* (Paris, Hachette, 1996).
*58.*  Dumazeau, Henri, *'La Condition humaine' — Malraux* (Paris, Hatier, 1970).

59. Hiddleston, James A., *Malraux: 'La Condition humaine'* (London, Edward Arnold, 1973).

60. Jenkins, Cecil, 'Introduction' to André Malraux, *La Condition humaine* (University of London Press, Textes Français Classiques et Modernes, 1968), pp.9–44.

61. *Malraux 'La Condition humaine'*, ed. Alain Cresciucci (Paris, Klincksieck, Parcours Critique, 1995).

62. Mercoyrol, Yannick and Richard Robert, *Premières leçons sur 'La Condition humaine' d'André Malraux* (Paris, Presses Universitaires de France, 1996).

63. Meyer, Alain, *'La Condition humaine' d'André Malraux* (Paris, Gallimard, Foliothèque, 1991).

64. Moatti, Christiane, *'La Condition humaine' d'André Malraux: poétique du roman d'après l'étude du manuscrit* (Paris, Lettres Modernes, 1983).

65. ——, *'La Condition humaine' — André Malraux* (Paris, Nathan, 1991).

66. Phalèse, Hubert de, *Les Voix de 'La Condition humaine' d'André Malraux à travers les nouvelles technologies* (Paris, Nizet, 1995).

*ON CHINESE HISTORY*

67. Bianco, Lucian, *Origins of the Chinese Revolution 1915–1949* (Stanford University Press, 1971).

68. Isaacs, Harold R., *The Tragedy of the Chinese Revolution* (Stanford University Press, 1961).

69. Phillips, Richard T., *China Since 1911* (Basingstoke and London, Macmillan, 1996).

70. Wei, Betty Peh-T'i, *Shanghai: Crucible of Modern China* (Oxford University Press, 1990).

*ADDENDUM*

*GENERAL STUDIES*

71. *André Malraux: Across Boundaries*, ed. Geoffrey Harris (Atlanta and Amsterdam, Rodopi, 2000).

72. Larrat, Jean-Claude, *André Malraux* (Paris, Librairie Générale Française, 2001).

73. Todd, Olivier, *André Malraux, une vie* (Paris, Gallimard, 2001).